Endorsements

"Mike Russell and Trisha Michael, along with the wisdom of Archangel Raphael (spoken through Trisha), free us from our self-imposed bonds. All our answers to our highest self, and our deepest desires are within, we just need the tools, and more so the courage to do the work. This book offers the beautiful, loving inspiration of Trisha, the strength and grounding of Mike, with the added blessing of Archangel Raphael. I highly recommend this book for those with the desire to obtain higher consciousness without losing their grounding."
~ Jennifer Ott, author and host of *The Super Jenius Show* on the Artist First Radio Network

"*A Journey of Discovery through Intuition with Help from the Angels* is a uniquely perfect place for someone longing to learn more about the spiritual path and how to access his or her intuition. The rich conversations with angels and the personal stories provide nice step-by-step processes that are easy to understand. If it's time for you to take the leap and connect more with your higher self, this is a good place to start."
~ Lori S. Rubenstein, JD, PCC, author of
Forgiveness, Heal Your Past and Find the Peace You Deserve

Trisha has the incredible ability to channel loving and uplifting wisdom from Archangel Raphael. Trisha and Mike are a powerful example of following one's Destiny—even when it doesn't make "sense," even when you can't see the whole picture—and this book is a manifestation of that faith, of that Love, of their individual and combined Destiny's."
~ Heather Kristian Strang, spiritual guide and author of
A Life of Magic: An Oracle for Spirit-Led Living

A Journey of Discovery

through Intuition

with Help from the Angels

Norma (Patsy)
Follow your dreams into your divine destiny! ♡
Angel hugs ♡
Trisha

Follow your heart - Enjoy and climb the Stairway to your own Absolute Love
Mike

Trisha Michael

Mike Russell

A Journey of Discovery
through Intuition
with Help from the Angels

Copyright © 2016 Trisha Michael and Mike Russell

ISBN: 978-0-9965785-7-8
ISBN: 0-9965785-7-9
Library of Congress Control Number: 2016937403

Cover design: Miko Radcliffe
Space photo: Courtesy of NASA
All images created by: Mike Russell
Poems written by: Mike Russell

Sacred Life Publishers™
SacredLife.com
Printed in the United States of America

Dedication

We would like to dedicate this book to all of our children, who through the years saw us in a greater light and loved us no matter what. Also, we would like to dedicate this to our dear Angel friend who patiently waited until he could weave us back into a partnership that would work towards spreading his messages of love and forgiveness.

~ Trisha and Mike

Contents

The Union of Trisha, Mike, and Archangel Raphael

Trisha's Intuitive Journey

To know love . . .
To share love . . .
To be in love . . .

These three items have been my heart's deepest wishes since I was ten. I fell in love with reading romance novels just to have my dream of knowing love, sharing love, and being in love come true, even if only in the pages of a story. When I was young and scared of being in life, I would count on my fingers the five things I loved over and over again, which are family, friends, reading romance novels, prayer, and nature. Growing into the intellectual part of my brain, I started slowly to forget my desire to be in love eternally. As I started to fill into my body, I became in love with the process of achieving straight A's in life. And yes, I achieved those straight A's. My intellect was driving my heart and body and I was applauded for my successes. I graduated in the top ten of my high school class as well as in the top percentage of my college class. I married my right intellectual match, and I had three brilliant sons. But I was unfulfilled in my heart and in my Spirit. I continued to pray the rosary and talk with my friends about God and about eternal love, which were pieces of my true love from childhood.

As I prayed for understanding the mystery of unconditional love through knowing, sharing, and being in love, I moved with my family from Little Falls, New York, to Portland, Oregon. I was hired by a bank that had a branch in a supermarket, where I met Mike Russell, who was the new branch manager and who became the cornerstone of my freefalling into Spirit and unconditional love.

Mike Russell was a unique manager who empowered his staff through the principles of positive thought. I was becoming aware of my mental and emotional fields and of how these fields ripple to create the world around us. Now my intellect was engaged in bigger principles of being the center of my experiences. The core identity of me started to change in such amazing ways. My life was more vibrant, and more alive. I knew that I was following my heart to my dream of knowing, sharing, and being one with unconditional love.

One beautiful spring morning as I was driving to a meeting singing aloud to Tina Turner's song "What's Love Got to Do with It" I was also demanding "God" to prove love to me. Be careful what you ask for. That afternoon while taking a break, I was standing outside with a group of co-workers. The day was lovely: the blue sky clear, and the sun was warm. We were all happy to take a break and soak into the hug of nature. While looking into the sky we all together noticed a group of birds in perfect synchronized flight. What a joy to see these birds flow in perfect motion. My whole being was pulled by their magical movement. Suddenly the birds swirled around in front of me, and down came an Angel who slowly became three-dimensional and solid in front of me.

Being brought up Catholic and loving the story of Fatima, I immediately went to my knees. The Angel spoke into my heart, telling me to have peace and that all was well. The next thing I was given was a revelation of heaven. All is well for all is Absolute Love. The wholeness of heaven was astounding and beyond the comprehension of all my previous conditioning. I saw all the people I loved and had judged as perfect and whole. The vibrations of Absolute Love went through me like waves, allowing me to know myself as perfect and whole.

Then the Angel put imprints of future events in my mind. I was not to become a prophet, but I needed to know that what I saw, what I felt, and what I heard was real, not just something glorified from my imagination. Finally, I heard the

Angel say, "You will be gifted with a baby girl," and then the Angel was gone.

I believe that time stood still during my Angelic visitation. Once the Angel left, the co-workers surrounding me asked if I had tripped and if was I okay. I immediately said that no, I had not tripped and, no, I was not OK. I started shaking and feeling nauseated. I went to the bathroom, locked myself in, and threw up for the next hour. My body did not want to stop shaking, and I did not want to forget the Angel. I finally lay on the cool floor and allowed my body to anchor back into Mother Earth. My coworkers wanted to call my husband, but he was so science oriented that I knew he would reject my experience as a physical reaction to a sugar condition because I never ate a lot throughout the day.

Once I was more settled, I drove home and then shared my experience with my husband. True to his personality, he wanted to drive me to the emergency room to have my blood drawn and checked. It was sad to me that my Angel was being explained away as a blood sugar problem and that I was hallucinating. I decided to just go to bed.

The next morning, I called my mother. My mother, being a very traditional Catholic, thought that I had been visited by a demonic being and that I needed to call a priest. I knew I saw, felt, and heard Absolute Love. No, I did not need an exorcism. I called a good friend who lived down the road, who told me that the Angel was a sign that I needed to accept Jesus as my savior. I had always loved Jesus. My revelation of heaven had shown me that we are all saved but that we have forgotten how whole and perfect we are. With a heavy heart I connected with my best friend, Wanda, who finally believed in my being visited by the Angel. She shared some books about near-death experiences that gave me peace about going to heaven and back. With Wanda, I was able to go to intuition classes and receive intuitive readings from others. Through these resources, I learned that my Angel was real, that I was not crazy, and that I would have my baby girl.

My day-to-day life after the Angel was not easy. Through the waves of Absolute Love, all my intuitive senses opened instantly. I was hearing Spirits, seeing Ghosts, and connecting with people's loved ones who had died. My eyes now saw people as colorful energy fields, not as bodies. I was afraid to talk about my new reality because I scared people with the messages that spontaneously came out of my mouth. My normal logical intellectual self of holding the elements of home, husband, kids, work, and friends together cracked beyond repair. What was normal? I did not know.

A couple of months after the Angel's visitation, I was making a bank deposit at Mike Russell's branch. I saw that Mike was alone at his desk and strongly felt the need to share about the Angel. When I sat down, he said, "You look like crap." Between the tears, I told him about the Angel. What a huge relief it was for me when Mike told me that he truly believed my story and would create a position at his branch to help me become more stable in understanding my gifts from the Angel while not fearing about losing my job. During the three years I worked for Mike, I learned how to incorporate and blend my gifts to be a guiding light in any situation life was bringing me. Also, during this time my baby girl, Julia, was born into my family.

After leaving banking, I became more and more devoted to my spiritual energy healing business. I grew in all my intuition skills and started offering classes, healing groups and sessions. Every now and then Mike and I would weave back into each other's lives to share our love of spiritual subjects. I knew our friendship had a Divine purpose, and was never fully conscious of the big picture.

When his beautiful wife Barbara transitioned to heaven, Mike reentered my life as a client and a friend in need. As Mike healed he went off to integrate this new phase of his life and to find his own new sense of normal. I was always joyful for the depth of friendship we shared.

One day, I saw an e-mail from Mike saying he wanted to write a book about me, the Angel, and my intuitive gifts. Wow, how scary it was to be exposed to the world. I was not fully comfortable to be under scrutiny of the public, especially as a single mom. I decided to wait to answer Mike, allowing Spirit to give me a clear sign of saying yes to this book project. A month later Mike e-mailed me again asking me if I was blowing him off. Actually, yes I was. I called Mike and the moment I heard his voice, I got full body goose-bumps and knew without a doubt that we were to write the book.

Love infused every step of our journey in creating the book, expanding our friendship into husband and wife, and diving deeper and deeper into our spiritual commitment in Absolute Love. The deeper that Mike and I allowed ourselves to free-fall into Absolute Love, the stronger Spirit showed up in our lives.

While writing the book with Mike, Archangel Raphael was showing up more and more in my daily card readings. I remember a channeler telling me that I had a contract to channel Archangel Raphael. When she told me this, her words made my heart sing with joy. However, I put this channeling contract on the back burner of my life. I wanted to feel somewhat normal in my Spirit led life. I did not want to appear to be the woo-woo of the woo-woos or crazy in any way. Could I stay grounded, safe, secure, and fully surrender into being a clear channel for Archangel Raphael? Yes, I could surrender to channeling Archangel Raphael, for I have been given the steps of the stairway to Absolute Love and trust all my senses.

One afternoon while resting in Mike's energy, Archangel Raphael spontaneously came through using my voice sharing the Divine contract Mike and I created before we came into form. Mike and my belief in "Love Is Enough" holds the clear channels for bringing and sharing this holy message of love and forgiveness. We are woven together, and our love opens new doors of experiences. Love is our story for beginning to end. As overwhelmed, surprised, and honored as Mike and I were at the first channeling of Archangel Raphael, we are now dedicated to "Love Is Enough" and to stepping into the bigger picture of our love story.

~ Trisha

Mike's Intuitive Journey

Trisha came for a visit and approached my desk where I was the branch manager of a local bank, and as I looked up,

I was surprised by the image that I was seeing. I immediately said, "What happened to you? You look like crap." Normally I would not say something like that to anyone, but Trisha and I went back years—we had worked for the same bank and I had hired her twice already for the different branches that I managed. So in this case, even though I was surprised I said that even in jest, I meant it from one friend to another.

She proceeded to tell me the story of the Angel coming to her and of how afterward she was having a hard time maintaining the current position as an assistant manager at another branch. For reasons obvious to me at the time, it seemed to me that having an Angel come visit in a three-dimensional capacity probably could make someone question everything, and it would be hard to function in any capacity. I remember saying that I completely believed her and it did not even cross my mind that this woman was losing it and needed help. Of course, her experience was real.

Looking back, I have a hard time explaining it, but I know now that I was using my own intuition to understand something that seemed impossible. My reaction was to offer her a job on the spot for a position that did not exist. I was just going to make one up. As I write this, no one can tell me that I was not being guided myself to believe in a friend, and offer a hand.

As things became easier for Trisha through her studying and trying to understand what had happened with the Angel and the skill set handed to her, I noticed that the branch itself changed in a way that I can only describe as loving and peaceful. I noticed that for the most part, the staff enjoyed Trisha's spiritual insights; many discussions were taking place, and it really was a wonderful place to work at the time.

Funny things would happen, such as when Trisha saw one of our deceased clients come into the branch, sit in the waiting area, and read the paper. My first reaction was to go and sit down in the same area just to see if I could feel anything. Now come on, who does that? But again I was finding that I was fascinated in exploring the unknown myself. This gave us a lot to talk about over time, and the staff found it entertaining as well. In fact, they would have

Tarot card parties after I went home for the day to my family. I have to admit that in all the years that I was in banking, this was the most interesting period of my career.

Eventually, as always, things change; Trisha went on to a new job, and I changed careers to become a lender at a friend's brokerage. Our friendship continued but not on a daily basis as it had been. We would occasionally talk after months had gone by, just catching up with what was going on in our jobs and families. It wasn't until the death of my wife, Barbara, and I was on my personal journey of grief that I was encouraged to reach out for some healing. By this time, Trisha had a healing business, running it out of her home, and I can now say that the Angels encouraged me through a discourse at the time of being in a fog and because of that, I guess I was more accepting.

Grief is different for everyone, and I can only really say what happened to me, but during the recovery stages of building myself back up, I would attempt to go for walks, which started out very short with my dog and ended up stretching to six miles. This definitely wasn't overnight, but a lot of things were happening to me that I can now say had a spiritual connection. For instance, for someone who never cared one iota about poetry, while I was walking one day, verses came in to my head; they would not leave me alone until I wrote them down. Sometime in this period, I started writing a blog because, again, thoughts and messages kept popping into my mind and I had to write them down. During this time, I was in such a fog of grief that doing this didn't seem too odd or not normal.

Then one day a message came in loud and clear that I needed to contact Trisha about writing a book about her and all the skills she has developed both before and after the Angel's appearance. I remember tripping and saying, "You have to be kidding. I do not know anything about writing books, and I am just trying to get myself on track." I pushed the thought away and tried to ignore it. But over the course of a month and many attempts from whoever wanted this to happen, I gave in and e-mailed Trisha about this silly idea. At the time, I felt that if I just followed through and did what was suggested, they or it would leave me alone.

It worked for quite a while. I did not think about it again until about four weeks later when I was reminded that I had not heard from Trisha and that I need to contact her again. I did not want to go through another round of repeated messages so I did what I was told and reached out to Trisha. If I remember right, she said she was still thinking about it and was not sure that she was the right person to have a book written about her. I told her the whole story, and guess what? She believed me without hesitation. Go figure. So we set up our first meeting to discuss the book and worked on the basic concepts once a week for the next six months. I went into it not even knowing what the subject matter really was, but over time, I found it so fascinating that I knew that somehow it had to get out to other people.

Spirit moving in mysterious ways comes to mind when I think about the weaving of Trisha's and my intuitive stories. But really, what is so mysterious about it? Two lives coming together many times through the centuries with what I would guess is a contract agreed to prior to bring light and love into a world that so needs it. My guess is that there has always been a common thread sewn through these two stories. Intuition has and always will be a direct connection to Spirit and I want to believe that Trisha and I have always had this connection. Normal lives with the ebbs and flows of life's unpredictable adventures do not always produce the outcomes chosen before coming to this earth. But I guess that sometimes those lives do work, and they go on to complete the mission intended.

Even though we cannot be sure that Trisha and I have been tied to Archangel Raphael and his message of love and forgiveness in our many past lives, through the intuitive senses and energy fields that we all have, we have been given the honor of completing a mission that we know and feel is one that we have chosen to partake in this time around. It is in that light that we accept the ups and downs of our two forms and know that we are in the perfect place at any moment and feel privileged that we are able to participate and promote this message that Love Is Enough, and we will continue to follow the signs of intuition that have been generously given to us.

In a time when spirituality seems so important but is not easy to find and hold onto, people, in general, are searching. They are searching for what can be described as their "self" and how they can and should relate to what is going on around them. This search for answers sometimes leads them to think that spirituality is something just out of their reach and something that will always elude them. Now, come what I call the "knowledge seekers." Knowledge seekers have existed throughout time; we sense that changes might be coming, and we intuitively want to be part of the solution and not the problem. That you have picked up this book shows that you, too, are a knowledge seeker. So, as a knowledge seeker, what can you do that has not necessarily been done before that will help you go to the new frontier and find this self with the knowledge that will help you achieve greatness not only for yourself but for those around you as well?

For centuries, books focused on spiritual development through one modality or another have been written. Usually the author is very specific, intending to give the reader an experience within a particular discipline. What Trisha has accomplished in this book is putting together the many methods she has developed and learned over many years of study and working with the Angels.

Twenty years have passed since I met Trisha, and since then, I have watched her ever-expanding knowledge grow. Her story, which includes growing up in a very Catholic family in Upstate New York, is pretty typical for children who have intuitive skills. As with most children, the adults around them push the innocence of feeling Spirit right out of them—or at least have them hide the skills that come naturally to all of us as we enter this Earth space. This was the case for Trisha throughout her school years, her travels, and her marriage until confronted by an Angel in three dimensions. This one event so influenced Trisha that from that moment forward, she was no longer able to ignore or hide her mission of giving perfect love to the world.

In one flash of brilliance, this Angel downloaded all potential intuitive skills and healing modalities as well as other information Trisha would need to take her on a twenty-year journey of books, classes, and training. Of course, this kind of heavenly download does not come without consternation. As with most changes this deep, Trisha's path deviated from some of those around her, but this path was hers before she arrived here, woke to this realization, and put her where she is today. To me, what Trisha has done is like a recipe for cookies. You take all the different ingredients that do not necessarily seem like they would fit together, mix them, and bake them into this really amazing, beautiful delicacy. Everyone wants a taste, but some push it away because they are afraid of what it will do to them. Since Trisha's epiphany, she has acquired these different ingredients from various sources and has mixed them to create the truly unique healer that she is.

This book can be used like a textbook in achieving higher awareness of Self and the process of healing using intuitive skills that can be achieved by everyone. It can also simply be read as the personal journey of someone truly inspired to do this work. I believe that you will find that it is all of the above as well as a whole lot more. I have faith that you will be able to use this book to learn multiple modalities of communication and will be able to create for yourself another source of light with which you can achieve greatness.

The skills developed in these books can be used individually, but most important, they can be combined to give you, the reader a way to coordinate the different skills. If nothing else, the journey will be interesting and fun, and you will not regret having read the story. Enough skills are presented in this book so that you, the reader, can achieve success and check yourself by focusing on the skills that work the best for you. Then over time, work on those areas in which you need more development. This book is written from the viewpoint of Trisha Michael and her connection to the Spirit world through her feedback from the Angels. At times, she speaks from her years of experience; at other times, she channels the Angels.

May the light shine on you, may you go home in peace when the time comes, and may you enjoy the reason that you are here.

~ Mike

Archangel Raphael's Welcome

We join you today to introduce as you say the purpose of why one as you would want to or have the willingness to consider reading the words on the pages that will go after this moment that I speak. We invite those already called to read this book, for it is part of their predestination, and this information is given to you in the format that Trisha and Mike are bringing. The information, of course, is to stimulate an awareness of the complete oneness you are at every moment. As you read these words, they will trickle down into the light memories that you hold within your deepest knowledge of your truth. Each chapter offers a way of becoming in touch with the light that is. The work of remembering your completeness within Absolute Love is an encounter of great joy. Many souls have been focused on this journey ever since coming into form or into human form.

The journey back is the consistent souls who keep on keeping on in their willingness to know the full light spectrum they hold. Clarity unfolds as each experience flashes a new lightness or exposure of pure oneness.

Trisha Michael, also known as My Lady—no words in any language could express the essence of your light. The brilliance of the colors is deeper than any stone you have witnessed. To seek the brilliance of you is daunting. To bath in the brilliance of you is magnificence. The depth of wholeness is the foundation of the awakening path that the ones who read will feel planted in. The seeds of who your readers will become are already stored in this wholeness. Coming to read these pages will help readers blossom. In each chapter, nourishment for one's mind, body, and soul, is woven and delivered in a soulful song.

Mike Russell is known as the Knowledge Seeker. The quest of truth is the compass you have been holding this time around. Your journey to yourself has brought a channel of purpose for yourself and others to know strength of choice for you knowledge seeker. Your seeking is like a rope as you throw it out to climb to new viewpoints of yourself and that of vision and family. Your determination in seeking benefits is your core essence, for it helps in seeking truth and knowing the truth fields.

A core reaction of strength, courage, and love will generate support, unconditional love, and ease for those around you. The action of your core is safe and will provide a clean path for awakening for you. Experience of your knowledge will help you to receive and give this knowledge to others. For you are here now to impart, explore, and deliver the full observations and conclusions of the information you have undertaken to deliver to others. My Lady might be a postwoman, but you are more the newspaper delivery boy, for you bring it more to the everyday people.

Beloved ones who are willing to open their minds, their hearts, and their awareness to explore and create a new awareness for themselves, this book will be a delightful and inspiring remembrance to tickle the light and love in wholeness in who you truly are in the oneness of love that is eternal. In Divine Love, all is holy. Enjoy the read, undertake the lessons, anchor the outcomes of the experiences, and believe deeper in the light that you are.

Blessings to you.

~ Archangel Raphael

Going Inside

Holding a clear mind, and
creating the space to connect to
Divine Love.
Absolute love holds so much unseen,
but can be felt when deep
within the space set aside.
Letting go of the clutter and
focusing on one thing,
can set your whole life
on the path of empowerment.

~ Mike Russell

Intuition

Intuition is being in tune to your highest aspect of yourself. Every time you meditate and every time you pray, you are cleaning the vibration between your highest self and your ego self so that you can be in tune. Intuition is being in tune to your highest aspect because you all have the answers already. Intuition feels random at times, and you think, "Why am I doing this or that?" Yet, that hunch, that gut feeling, or that knowing is you being in tune to the highest need that you came to this earth to express.

So the object of intuition is "How I can tune myself to the highest aspect of myself, which is already being hugged in love, to be as clear as it can be?" Thus, you know, without a doubt, that it is what you can do to create heaven on earth. We are looking at the gift of "as above, so below," or what you know as yourself above is now brought to you here. "As within, so without," so that you can take action outward from what you know without a doubt.

Intuition builds like a GPS unit within your heart. It is your "God-positioning unit" that helps you know with certainty that each step you take is what you are supposed to be doing. Sometimes life seems out of order, or without definition, but because you know that what you are doing is right in your heart, then it is your truth to follow.

~ Archangel Raphael and Trisha Michael

Introduction

Knowledge seekers ask how they can feel comfortable entering an unknown space and determining how to create a strong base from which to apply so many new skill sets without being overwhelmed.

We are here to share our knowledge and expansion of our intuition. In doing so, creating a safe community should be emphasized because intuition is a very intimate space that we invite people into. So in that time of intimacy with each other, we need to keep it very safe and recognize that what we say does not leave the space around us and that we hold the trust and integrity of our words and thoughts with not only each other but with anyone that we can communicate with through intuitive skills. If you do not feel safe, then you will not get what you want from an intuition course or book. So we offer these guidelines for creating a safe place:

- In this space, there will be only open minds and open hearts. You will be embraced for who you are. You are invited to share in all activities. This is a space where you are loved and accepted.
- This is a space to explore your truth without judgment. All sharing is held sacred. You participate when your heart sings with joy.
- Learning is your journey. All learning styles are honored, for your gifts are uncovered when you feel safe to give and receive of equal energy.
- This is a place to be fully honest with yourself to uncover your truths and remember the power of your truths as you share them in everything that you do.

- Each person in this space contributes in his or her way to hold the wholeness that we share at this moment.

Created by Mike Russell

Our foundation for learning and growing our intuitive skills is trusting that we are safe to explore outside of our physical reality. Once we are fully anchored in being safe, we then build our stairway to Absolute Love. The foundation steps in building our stairway to the Source are two core beliefs. The first core belief is that Source is Absolute Love.

In Absolute Love there is and only ever will be Absolute Love. No negativity, no fear, and no separation exist in the source, for the source is and always will be eternally Absolute Love. All the worries of your conscious mind can be put at ease if you stay in touch with the two foundation steps that begin the stairway to Absolute Love.

Our second core belief is that we—meaning humans—and we—meaning all elements in form around us—are created through Absolute Love. In this creation, our perfection is our natural state. Having all the gifts of the Source in the creation of us, we can then join heaven on earth to create clarity with our intuition.

Using the belief that perfection is the natural state, you will recognize that the person before you came with his or her own Divine blueprint, and what that person is doing is a dance through that Divine blueprint. You can accept his or her actions because you are perfect. You have to understand it from your perspective but understand that, for that person, it is perfect.

Chapter 1

The Alpha: Laying the Groundwork

What Is the Source?

Knowledge seekers search for meaning to the beginning,
how religion and spirituality can work together,
and how they can fit into the puzzle of life.

The Source is Absolute Love. Within Absolute Love, there is no guilt, shame, blame, fear, and separation. All is perfect, all is one, all is eternal, and all is whole. We were all whole, perfect, and one.

When the Angel came to me, I felt and saw Absolute Love. In this love, there is no space for fear, evil, hatred, guilt, or shame. At the time, I was experiencing many of these emotions because of my upbringing. Through my ego, my human mind could not believe that this was so. The Angel shared with me his perfection and how his Divine placement in my life gave me the moral muscles to believe in something more. Later, I saw my ex-husband in Absolute Love. Yes, my ex-husband is part of wholeness and part of Absolute Love.

Who are we?
We are Spirit.
We are Absolute Love.
We are whole.
We are perfect.
We are created from one source: Absolute Love.

Yes, you are perfect, for you are part of all. Perfection is our natural state. Perfection extends all that you are as you naturally move and as you naturally partake of the landscape around you. Your natural state is what comes easily for you from the inside out. Your talents, your temperaments, your joy, your dreams, and your Divine blueprint are all what you are here to share.

My perfection is just being me: being happy, being silly, being loving, and being honest. The Angel showed me how my perfection radiates from all that I am in my inner being to all whom I share my energy with, brightening their light on their perfection.

Ego, on the other hand, is the lack of Absolute Love. The root belief of separation is our ego, which employs denial, repression, projection, hate, fear, and scarcity, to name a few. The ego seeks to resolve problems not at the source but "out there" somewhere, and it gains strength from more separation. In the book *The Disappearance of the Universe,* Gary Renard says that through a split mind, the ego is born. Duality is a result of the belief in separation, and a world of good, bad, love and fear materializes.

The source, Absolute Love, gives to us all its attributes. We create this dream, this illusion, and this duality of time and space with a tiny thought of "What if . . . ?" What if we usurp the Source? In a moment of madness, we create separation. With our full power, we create the root cause of all our stress by deciding that something is wrong, bad, or evil.

We create our dual reality. Deep in our ego mind, we create and firmly believe that we will awaken from our dual reality, from this madness, through the gift of the Source and that the Divine communication device—the whole Spirit—will be our handrail in light and love as we climb the stairway to Absolute Love. When we trust our Divine communication, we fully engage in the big what-if. What if we are perfection, whole in Absolute Love, now and forever?

When I started building my trust in the core belief that perfection is my natural state, I was taking a class at a community college to learn basic computer principals. In the class, my teacher kept saying to us, "You are perfect." To that, I would say, "Yes, I am perfect. Thank you." Each time I said that I was perfect, in my mind, I was rewriting my *I am a disappointment* ego script because I remembered my truth: I was created in Absolute Love, and my perfection was, and always will be, my natural state.

After class one day, a woman who sat behind me said, "How pretentious of you to always reply back to the teacher, 'Yes, thank you. I am perfect.'" I said to her that no, it was my right to claim my perfection, for if I can trust in my perfection, then the work of all before me is perfect. As you claim your perfection, the world before you is perfect to be anchored in the full gift for us to create our Divine blueprint that is our perfection for this life that we are in now.

The Alpha and Omega

What do we mean by the "alpha and the omega"? When we have made the decision to incarnate to any form, our goal then is to go back to the formlessness of Absolute Love. Consider it the beginning and the end. Some people call it the descent into hell or into some type of body or into the ego. People always choose lessons that make them really go into their ego or their negative thoughts. What you are looking for in this process is growth. Growth is always about self-love and Divine Love, and going back to the perfection that you know you are. So by going inward through meditation and focusing on Divine Love through whatever means you feel comfortable with, you may feel and see it in your energy field. Some people see it in their third eye as an open white canvas.

Whatever paradigm you use, you may feel the Divine Love in every cell by having it register on every level of your consciousness, subconsciousness, and superconscious spaces. That is truly who you are, and you can claim it through your meditation. As within, so without. You can project that person outward to everyone; then, before you know it, events are not separate entities because Divine Love becomes the paint that the outward projection becomes, connecting all things. It opens up the outside world to you in all its vibrancy and radiance.

We can never fully understand ours or another's alpha and omega. We all grow by holding Divine Love and Divine Light. People are a spectrum of connection and separation. Offering others grace and space to be, you can connect in love with others. Love's connection will spark within them and within you. The more you connect in love, the more plugged in you are to remembering the oneness. When you reach that spiritual high, all of your relationships, with yourself and with others, will become more intimate.

Divine Love is a perfect place. In it, I have not seen an event that is not perfect for anybody regarding his or her alpha and omega. I step back and watch what is going on. I do not have to take anything personally. I am working on my triggers so that I can be a divine instrument to facilitate the healing. If I did not do all my inner journey work, I might take something personally, but now I can say, "You are mistaken," and not take it personally. I am intrigued with their point of view and I see it as footnotes on the research paper. It becomes an "Oh yeah. Maybe I will write it in, or maybe I will not." So by not taking something personally, you keep your ego into check. If you do your meditations, you are separating yourself from the ego. This is perfect. This is where the healing comes in. You have changed the perception of the event to know it is perfect. The healing now is perfect.

You magnetize the inner beauty of you. Your core desires and needs are brought to you with ease and grace, holding the joy in each moment.

Religion and Spirituality

Religion and spirituality usually come up for individuals working and honoring their connections with the subconscious mind, the superconscious mind, and oneness in Absolute Love. All religion and all spirituality are part of the whole. All truths are part of us and part of how we want to remember. We are now one in love, which is our choice for experiencing our reality.

When I was born, I saw everything around me as moving dots of lights. When I was three, I broke my leg twice, which led me to a deep understanding of how solid this world appears. When I went to church school at five, and the nun told me, "God is everything and everywhere, and God is omnipotent and all present." I knew that was absolutely true, for I saw all in the lights of Spirit, and we all were part of this brilliant life.

To explain truths outside of our physical senses and outside of our human comfort zones, we create religious or spiritual vehicles, the structures to hold and nourish the lights I have seen since I was born. Being uniquely individual in our journey home, we find and fill the vehicle that fits. For me, a good analogy is we all drive different cars to arrive at a destination or home. Each car has a defining structure or attribute that makes you feel safe and helps you enjoy the ride. Each vehicle makes a statement to you and others about how you want to experience the ride of life. Many elements of all vehicles are the same. There are differences, yes. But are the differences so extreme that you cannot make the journey home to love? Thus, all structures celebrating the journey home to Absolute Love have Divine Truths. You are free to choose the vehicle, be it religious or spiritual, for your journey to be fully connected to your Creator.

So, where do you begin and I end? Each person is different. Once you learn to drive, you can figure out how to drive any vehicle. Yes, we are more alike than not. Once you look beyond the body recognizing the energy frequencies we are all alike. Separation no longer exist. We are always comingling. Take time to watch people, and you will see how very similar and connected we are to each other.

Devoting time to some type of meditation and/or prayer every day is very important especially when you are starting out. While growing up in the Catholic Church, I said the rosary every night with my family. So when I started in this work, I would do the rosary every morning and sometimes twice in one day. Saying the rosary was a great meditation for me to organize and clear my mind to hold perfect love. Meditation and or prayer is addicting in activating the fullest feeling of love's connection and achieving the clearest message for yourself and others.

Owning Your Divine Essence

Owning your divine essence is holding the truth that you are Spirit, whole, and innocent. The point of your wholeness is the perfect love that you are within, which is Absolute Love, and that we are one. To really own that truth is very scary, and people sabotage this love instead of embracing it because when we are incarnated here, into the world of bodies, we think we have left perfect love. What we have done is fall into a dream of not being whole in love.

So owning your divine essence is bringing forth everything we have experienced with our intention, meditation, and being mindful. Now you are an active creator with Absolute Love. You are trusting your life's journey with the connective dance of the whole divineness of the holy power and presence of oneness in love that you truly are.

What happens is that we create the world of form through the gift of free will, which is centered in the solar plexus, or third chakra. Our creator, Absolute Love, wholly gives us the gift of free will without conditions. As we create through this gift, we keep asking, "What if . . . ?" and the infinite energy responds, and finally, with our what-if questions, we usurp Absolute Love, and the infinite energy responds with total blackness, total loss, and death beyond all that we ever know. We create this separation from Absolute Love, and it explodes outward in billions on billions of pieces of separation. Absolute Love, or love without conditions, hugs us tightly back into the eternal beat of oneness. We only separated but for a moment, yet this moment for us is the world of form, giving us the experiences for remembering who we truly are.

Because of the great pain in our moment of separation, we believe we must childproof the gift of free will. As parents, we desire to keep our children and ourselves free from pain. Thus, we "childproof" the world around us so that we never experience pain again.

As individuals, we cannot hover around the ones we love twenty-four hours a day to make certain no harm happens to them. Ultimately with our desire to ask, "What if . . . ?" and the gift of free will, pain eventually happens. Once again, we get lost in the painful story of the booboos from our experience instead of comprehending the trust walk of being fully in charge of your choices and your creations. By owning our divine essence, we let go of the need, desire, and belief in childproofing anybody and anything in your landscape. Embrace the power of the gift of free will to create in the highest and best design of knowing Absolute Love. Once your free will is in total alignment with your divine essence, you easily connect your perfect puzzle of Absolute Love's embrace.

This is the most profound dance of life when you truly integrate everything around you into this welcoming embrace of your true essence of Spirit. Our logical mind, as we know, loves the scientific. Although this is very important in life too, our ability to take the logic and integrate it or zip it into the awakening of life fulfills our Divine Self.

Truly, the Divine helps you to understand not only where you perhaps have an ego attachment but also how you are creating a manifestation of that understanding of ego. Many times we will look at a negative situation and want to become the victim of it. But, really, that is exactly what we need. In every moment you are given what you need. When we take this ownership on and we recognize that it is part of our divine creation, then we can realize how this lovely life presents itself because we love drama in our world.

One day, I awoke, and Archangel Raphael had me meditate on a straight line, and it scared me. In life, a straight line means death. By plucking that line of eternity, he was showing me that the highs and lows create vibrations of perception that we understand in intervals of good and bad and that this perception creates our drama. We believe that we have to create from that placement of vibration because it somehow heightens our life and awareness of what we do. In fact, the opposite is true. Everything is playing off a continual straight line of love that creates your most lasting and sustainable effect. Through gratitude, we all then bow to the mastery of this event, life, or extension of love.

When we are born, we do not necessarily understand the process of life. The treasure of life is recognizing and analyzing first what pieces were given to you. We also do not get the complete picture. We do not know how we are tied in. Sometimes, we do not even believe that there might be a bigger picture. Somehow, we are given Divine assignments that, in our minds, feel totally random, as though we have somehow been left out. We cannot assume anything from the puzzle pieces we are given in life, so we need to come together to build our puzzle because your puzzle pieces interact with people. Others need your participation just as you need theirs.

Once we acknowledge how very similar we are despite our differences, it is time to heal what makes you feel separate. On your journey inward, you will look for what makes you feel alone, as though you are not enough, through shame, blame, pain, anger, hate, and victimized. Through meditation and/or prayer, you have greater clarity of the causes of your feelings of separation. Questioning your beliefs about why you feel this way and what caused it will give you a deeper connection to Spirit. As you clear your triggers—the causes of your separation—you can hold the space to be a divine instrument of Absolute Love.

I believe that holding a strong connection with the Holy Spirit means having clarity of mind. You must go inward on your journey, recognizing what makes you feel separated and question your beliefs. Believing that you are separate makes you think something is wrong when perfection is the natural state of everything. As you unite your thoughts and actions around the belief that "perfection is the natural state," you give yourself, "grace and space" when you are being triggered to have the perfection of the moment be shown to you, which allows your intuition the opportunity to bring forth insight from your truth and the comprehension of the whole perfect. How lovely to fully give and receive information with the highest aspect of love.

How many times have you come into someone's life and, despite not knowing his or her whole picture, made decisions about him or her from the few of puzzle pieces you could see and then held that person to that perception? You do not know that your piece could fit them. What we often expect is not necessarily what is, but it is what we need from other people's puzzle pieces.

We can become very engrossed in our own pieces thinking that they have to fit. That is why I love personal transformation and working with the Divine because there is a willingness to engage without the big picture. The Divine holds all of our prerequisites, predeterminations, and decisions that make up our puzzle. With our active participation with the Divine wholeness, we might not know instantly how to place specific puzzle pieces of our Divine blueprint, but we can trust that the placement will happen in Divine timing with the Divine connections of people, places, and events. Life becomes a movement of connecting, comprehending, and loving the big picture you are creating.

Puzzle Exercise 1

Find a small puzzle or a picture from a magazine that you can tear up into many pieces. If you are working with others, randomly hand out puzzle pieces without knowing what the picture looks like. If you are working by yourself, turn the puzzle box or picture over so you do not see the picture, and randomly shuffle the pieces.

As you build the puzzle or picture, consider how the pieces fit together, bringing the big picture together. Life is like this. Sometimes you think you have a piece in the right spot—for example, a job or a relationship—and then realize things in your life aren't fitting together. This one piece in the wrong place prevents the bigger picture of your life from forming.

If we did not all participate, a puzzle piece would be missing. We have to participate in life. We are all given puzzle pieces and need to recognize that together we create more.

Puzzle Exercise 2

In this exercise, get a more complicated puzzle with many pieces, but this time, it is OK to look at the puzzle box or picture. Many times what happens on earth is that we become so bogged down by our pieces. When we are young, the puzzle is easy, but as we get older, it gets harder. Our will be done is how we make decisions. We stop engaging and think that we can opt out of a divine course, thinking about how strong our free will is, and we let go of the thought that there is a Divine force in our life. We might choose to opt out of relationships. Owning your Divine essence is saying that your divine will can equal your free will. You can make great decisions while allowing your divine will to participate.

Now look at the picture of the completed puzzle on the box. What part pulls you in—the edges, a color, an element in the image? You are seeing that your free will and beliefs can work with your divine will. You are not overriding it. Your patterns of beliefs can be in conjunction with holding your perfect divine will. What we feel is lost will be found.

When we are guided, we cannot outrun our Angels or our Guides. They will keep up with you. All of a sudden you just see good falling into your lap, like the puzzle pieces coming together. No puzzle pieces are missing from your life. They are somewhere around you. We all need completion, and we need to see it in our lives. Every life is about building your divine puzzle. The more we own that we have a blueprint that we came in with, the better.

People die regretting that they did not complete the puzzle. They knew they had pieces all along that they never looked at. When we co-create with heaven, we are always saying, "Show me the divineness. Let me take on that puzzle piece. I have the tools now to participate, and I am willing to," and so it is!

Chapter 2

The Split Mind

*Knowledge seekers often wonder why
they appear to be separate and how they can
heal the separation to have a more
fully connected experience.*

The split mind is the land of the ego. The whole mind is eternal in Absolute Love. Because of the gift of free will, our moment of madness, which is our decision to separate from Absolute Love, created separation, duality, and the split mind. In the split mind, judgment is the king over good versus bad and love versus hate. No one is ever certain of his or her truths. Worry is a constant. Pain and pleasure become the lows and highs of each story told. Emotions play off others' judgments instead of being a force in your intent to love. The Holy Spirit created a new communication, weaving the conscious and unconscious mind that eliminates the belief of separation and holds wholeness as the constant of the one mind that is love.

Our bodies are just the playgrounds through which we get to experience duality, and the games that play out are wholly in our minds. Everyone on this planet is made up of the same building blocks. You and I are truly the same. Because of our split minds, we focus on perceived differences and allow those differences to provide the backdrop for these highs and lows and our trauma drama in our lives.

As you practice mindfulness in partnership with the Holy Spirit, you begin to heal your split mind into a whole one of love. You will feel calmer, more energized, more focused, and, possibly, a sense of light exploding in every cell.

Part of healing the split mind is recognizing that because we are in human form and our mind does hold onto the belief that we are split, we judge people and things. When we recognize this, we do not want to be guilty of judging others. Instead, what we need to do is acknowledge that we make judgments and observe ourselves from a more neutral place, saying, "Wow. What if everything were neutral, would I still judge (this person, situation, or item) as good or bad? What if this was a movie playing out and these were characters acting. How would I view it?"

Consider chalk. Chalk is needed to write on the chalkboard, but chalk left alone is neither good nor bad. By using chalk as a tool of communication of wisdom on the chalkboard, we claim it as good. Yet in another case, this same chalk used as a tool for graffiti on the downtown office building could then be judged as bad. Give chalk a break. At the end of time chalk is just chalk. Our judgment about the way the chalk is used as a tool of expression creates the stories of good and bad. Honestly, chalk is just chalk.

View your life as a reporter would, by taking the emotion, drama, and ego out of it. Much of our world is like an onion. Just when you think you peeled back one layer or issue, it shows up in a different place, and you discover that you have not really assessed and forgiven that issue completely. Becoming one with your split mind reality is like creating chicken broth from the chicken bones. After the mixture has cooked and you've removed bones, the fat separates, floating at the top. Underneath it, you have all this beautiful broth. This is how our mind is. As you release the layers, other things can come up. The chicken broth is the unconscious mind and the layer that you are sifting off is the conscious path stories being forgiven in light and love. Over time with mindfulness and forgiveness as pain comes up, it will lessen and lessen until it is not so painful.

Our unconscious minds are immense, but we are afraid of this because really deep down, our true cores are hidden in the unconscious mind, which is tethered to our light. The unconscious light is the true core being. We fear our light more than anything else. So, as we forgive those layers, we look at the pain around an event, removing all judgment and allowing us to claim our light. When you finally hit the core of the pain, because it is no longer part of the broth of your unconscious mind, your light will shine and those minerals will come up to the surface and you can finally know how loved you are.

In our oneness, our light of good, wholeness, and innocence has never stopped shining. We have just put many obstacles in its way from really shining. Our conscious mind is just the tip of the iceberg of our mind, yet we manifest and create from the vast unconscious mind because these thoughts are what bubble up. We have to keep looking at these thoughts until we fully create from the whole mind. People can sustain a short-term conscious intention of happiness, but they cannot do it for the long term because that conscious happiness is not fully connected to the command of the unconscious mind and to the core of our truth: our oneness in Absolute love.

Give yourself a break by giving yourself permission to feel more guilt or self-imposed punishment because you judge. Judging happens because a body, which is a tool of expression in our world of duality, is viewed as good or bad. Be kind to yourself as you heal the split mind through forgiveness. When you are always in the moment, you become aware of any good or bad thought and can immediately say, "Forgive, forgive, forgive." This active mantra is your gift for breaking the spell of separation and for your accepting that you are good inside and out. In forgiveness you love what is.

I love clouds. Watch clouds long enough, and you can see images form in them. You may see one that looks like an airplane, but then it dissipates. When you are mindful of your thoughts and their form, you can try mimicking the clouds. Allow those thoughts to form: Think, "How interesting" and then allow them to dissipate.

If you pay attention to how your thoughts form, you will get a good indication of where your true being really resides. Are you motivated by thoughts of fear, or are you motivated by thoughts of love? In choosing to motivate life through love, you create a better way of dancing with your painful and victimizing life experiences. In the long run, pain is no fun for anybody. It might give you instant attention, but that kind of special attention wears off. Sooner or later, people will tell you to get over your pain. When you finally command yourself to get over it from your core being, a better way appears. Your perfect path to healing appears.

With healing intentions, over time, your pain stories will come to the surface, exposing the darkness to light and providing you an opportunity to forgive. Each choice made in love and in light allows forgiveness, which eliminates your core fear of separation. All healing of your split mind allows your core light to shine.

We all hold this truth to be one in our light. We are part of this one goal together. Through the gift of the Holy Spirit, the dance of connecting our lights to shine on the darkness from the unconscious mind, we know the world of Absolute Love.

My powerful subconscious mind is constantly monitoring every facet of my existence, and I see how wonderfully it keeps me functioning in so many ways and on so many levels. The subconscious mind, transcending the conscious mind in so many ways, keeps all of my bodily functions perfectly tuned and intact. I would not know how to grow one hair on my head without it.

To get an idea of the relationship between the various areas of the mind, imagine a bull's-eye pattern. The smallest circle in the center represents the conscious mind, or the mind in which we spend most of our daily hours functioning while in contact with the so-called outer world. The subconscious mind is next, a larger and vaster circle surrounding the conscious. Here are all our memories of all our experiences of all our lifetimes. In this circle, we find the many categories of things that the subconscious mind is responsible for to keep functioning. The third circle on the bull's-eye would be the superconscious mind—our Highest Self, the mind most in touch with the Divine. All spiritual, mystical, and psychic experiences come from this circle.

Through the analogy of the bull's-eye pattern, it becomes obvious that for Holy Divine connections and impressions of information or light to reach the conscious mind in the center, it must pass then through the subconscious mind. Again, you can see the importance of the subconscious as you begin to see even the so-called negative experience in a positive light. And once again, your subconscious shows you that you have so-called good luck. But you see clearly that it is all of your own choosing and creation.

The powerful subconscious mind, containing all of this programming, can constantly be impressed and reimpressed on it. It can be changed, and belief systems can be reprogrammed through repetition and through repeated exposure to new programs that you may prefer to use to picture beyond yourself, in the outer world of form. So hold on to positive affirmations, truly believe them, and state boldly that you are in control and are no longer a victim. Remember that you are always in control of those things that occur and are likely to occur to you in the future, and when repeated with great feeling and depth, then your subconscious mind will begin to assimilate that truth.

Repetition is the key to reprogramming the subconscious mind. Eventually, like clay, your subconscious mind will, indeed, be remolded and reprogrammed. And then, as if by magic, the effects of the so-called outer world will begin to reflect this new programming, and your destiny will change and/or improve.

Separation, Duality, and Forgiveness

Many people believe that we are just our bodies and that we are just our physical senses. We see people's bodies, but where does a person begin and where do they end?

I was talking to Archangel Raphael, and when I said, "I was out of my mind," he replied, "No, Trisha. You are out of your body. You are one with the one mind of eternity." As I meditated on this statement, I realized how we all move from the mind. We respond to the intention and attend to the thoughts. We are spiritual energy beings, fueling our holy temple: our bodies. Because energy is everywhere and everything, we are one with everything.

Connecting with your intuition is looking beyond form and resonating with how truly one you are with everything.

Separation has given us the fuel for pain and pleasure. Pain is uncomfortable, and pleasure is never sustainable. Thus, we want to childproof someone's free will. You can never control another's free will. Interacting with people is always a simple invitation for them to dance with you to celebrate a remembrance of love and a remembrance of oneness. Yes, every moment is an invitation with the Holy Spirit to reach beyond what is comfortable to claim a renewal of your wholeness.

Because we can physically touch, hear, see, taste, and smell the fuel of separation—pain and pleasure—we believe in duality. Our bodies hold and continually register the impact pain and pleasure has on all that we do. We start choosing only what brings pleasure to our bodies, finding every creative way to numb pain. This game of giving and receiving pleasure and of numbing pain is a life in duality. Each movement is a transaction between pain and pleasure, good and bad, positive and negative, and love and hate. In this game, we all operate through our conditioning to access the world through our bodily senses.

Once you experience what is beyond your physical senses and body, your deep-rooted belief in separation will start to unravel. The more and more the experiences of your reality challenge your physical senses, the more you will question, believing that there must be more, and the more the Holy Spirit will reconnect you to the knowledge that you are the creator of this game of duality. As the creator of this vast, complex, ever-changing game, you will know for certain that you are not a victim of your reality. You are the conductor, bringing the expression of love or fear to each moment. Each moment and each choice is an intention in which you mindfully create from your truth: that you are Absolute Love.

The biggest gift to give yourself through knowing your connection to love is being present in each moment. Participating in acts of love big and small is truly addicting. Your destiny was to be part of this gift to humanity. Now is the time to give yourself permission to take baby steps in expressing love in each moment. By simply being you, you are already vibrating love from your core. This vibration creates in you the ability to act in love and not fear, judgment, and separation. Smile and the world around you will reflect your smile.

If I am taking anything personally, I say, "Forgive, forgive, forgive." Saying forgive three times allows you to forgive yourself, to forgive me, and to forgive whatever you are focused on. Forgiveness dissolves the void of separation, melting time and the game of duality. Forgiveness brings comprehension to our assumptions in fear, which makes false evidence appear real. We all make assumptions when comprehending and completing facts, data, and thoughts. We connect with others based on our assumptions of our reality. To step out of our assumptions is to question, question, and question our reality and all our beliefs holding our reality together. To question is to let go of any idea of now and to uncover your truth. If we do not know people's reason for being who they are at this moment, we do not know their alpha and omega. We do not know others' true purpose, yet we box them up in our reality based on our assumptions.

Because of our assumptions, we become righteous regarding things around us. I let people show me this through their energy, and I can see where they are really at right now. You are exactly where you need to be. Once you let go of your assumptions, people really feel safe to share their truth with you. Then your intuition is clean and clear. You can really read the person and give the highest and best part of him or her back.

In the game of duality, when you become mindful of infusing love to duality, you can exit any *good guy versus bad guy* situation you have constructed at any point. Once I am mindful that I am being the bully or the bad guy in an interaction and/or relationship, I can say in my mind, "Forgive, forgive, forgive." Then I stop my assumptions and righteousness and question my beliefs about the person or the situation until I know my truth. I understand and comprehend my behavior and can shine love throughout my alpha and omega to dissolve duality and know love eternally.

When you choose love and become diligent about doing so, you bring love to all players in your game of duality. You do not have to accept behavior that involved the continuation of pain. You do not have to hang out with the person to prove your love before you move on. You have made a contract to heal your assumptions about separating from this person because of what he or she is triggering in your life. Through forgiveness and seeing love in this person, you no longer have to play this game of pain. You may be destined to fight with some people, but by being clear in your love and remembering that everyone is one, you can love these people, see that they are acting from free will, and can forgive the contract. If one person no longer works against the other, then the game does not play out.

Get out of the world of reaction into the world of love. This makes time disappear. When you are forgiving and loving, you do not have to go through these negative places with people. If you do, you can say to yourself that this person's truth is not your truth with you and that you will not play the game. This decision supports both of you because no one has to go through the detour to get to love. You are always simultaneously a teacher and a student. So what does this person bring to you that makes you a student, even if he or she is yelling at you? Usually, as within, so without. Because we believe in duality, we do not see ourselves as just fully love. It is really hard to say that in every moment you are acting in love, but each step in love is the greatest gift to give.

To be awake is to see the Divine perfection in every moment, every breath, and every particle of matter and to know that you created something and that it is good. Yes,

Absolute Love hugged us in our moment of madness. In that Divine hug, we were blessed in the whole Spirit—"Holy Spirit"—to know and claim that we are all one. With the sparkles of light and love the Holy Spirit weaves, it mends and heals all our fears of separation with the act of forgiveness. You are forgiving that one decision of separation or the guilt of that decision—remorse.

When you forgive, you open space to feel Divine Love while working within every part of your awareness. Then events will happen, and suddenly, you are not going to act out in fear. You will say, "How interesting," and know that what is happening is just a reflection of yourself at the moment.

We come into our bodies, which are our holy temples, to experience and choose to experience love versus fear. So, in this experience, we create our syllabus to graduate. I see it as an outline or a table of contents in a book. You can call them spiritual chapters. So those chapters are pretty solid, and because those are the experiences you have called forth to walk through with forgiveness, you change the outcomes of those chapters.

If you give a speech multiple times and following an outline, each time you give the speech, the words change because you might tailor it to a specific audience. For example, I had a vision that I was going to hit one of my kids with a car. I have had these visions since I was fourteen. So, I never wanted to drive or have kids because I did not want to hit anyone with a car. For me, as that event neared, I have more and more visions about it. Because I had just finished reading *The Disappearance of the Universe* and was studying *The Course of Miracles*, by Dr. Helen Schucman, I kept doing forgiveness around myself. Every time I saw that event in my third eye, I would say, "Forgive, forgive, forgive." Saying those three words with intent would dissolve the energy around that event. So forgiveness in that perspective is used as a tool for changing the outcome. You can change the outcome in form. In doing that, what happened was on a dark night, my son got out of the car to get his bike. I saw him go by the house to get his bike, and I pulled back to take another son to the store. After looking for and not seeing anything, I heard a scream and a crunch at that point. Then my son was knocking on the car window and saying that I killed his bike. I said, "Hallelujah. I didn't kill my kid."

You still have to experience life because each event is a bullet point, but the outcome of these events will become so much easier, and you won't have to revisit them. You might have many endings, and the more you forgive it, it changes the ending to the least degree. I created this so I can change it. If I feel like I am experiencing separation, then I need to forgive.

What I love is recognizing—knowing—that the more we complicate things, the more we are in our ego. When we do not complicate things, we are in our purest form. *God* is just a noun and a verb. It is just that simple. We like to add all the adjectives, adverbs, pronouns and the expectations. I really know that my whole life is forgiveness. That is my true purpose and is why I am here. So as I forgive all the judging I do or have done, it is disappearing fear. Then more love and light can come in. I start and end my day with a prayer on forgiveness. You can use various sources to find prayers, or you can make up your own.

Connecting Exercise

If you are in a group setting, you stand and hold hands with those around you. Enhance your connection of mind, heart, soul, and cellular memories with each person celebrating the connection of your now. If you doing this exercise while you are alone, visualize a group of people that have connected in a meaningful way to you, and follow the same steps. Close your eyes, and take three deep breaths. Feel your heart beating with the person on your left and right. When you feel that synchronicity, open your eyes, look at each person, and say through your eyes, "I love you." Bow and look to your feet, invoking the cellular memory of all walks you have taken in your holy temple. You are sharing these memories with the group. You are now in an energy bubble that is beyond belief. This connection heightens remembering each other and how deeply we can share our feelings and memories when we anchor in the connection of our oneness. Bringing clarity to our intuition is to bring purity to the remembrance of oneness with everyone and everything. To know and anchor in oneness is the key to fully be you wherever you are.

Intuition

Use your light and be in tune to the whole of you. According to Wikipedia, "Intuition is knowledge gained of something without reasoning or the five basic senses. Throughout time, many of the great achievers have spoken of successful decisions they made based on hunches, insights, visions, and gut feelings. The word intuition comes from the Latin word intueri, which is usually translated as 'to look inside' or 'to contemplate.'"

In this process, you are using the five basic senses of sight, hearing, touch, smell, and taste and expanding them. For the most part, in our world, we are taught and are conditioned to believe that what we can touch, feel, see, and hear as fact or truth. The data we gather with our basic senses create the logic in our belief systems. Do not argue with the basic belief that one plus one equals two; if you do, all the other basic beliefs you have been taught might just crumble into a big junk file in the mind's processing system. Yes, I am poking fun at our perceptions of reality because in duality, all perceptions should be questioned.

As foundations and anchor points of awareness, our basic senses do give us a physical reality, a reality from and with our body, to interact in the world of form and gravity. I call it the "form world" because everything takes on a dense shape. As you work with the forms in the landscape that creates your environment, your basic senses will feel safe to expand, explore, and uncover all the layers of information within our reality. In a safe space, a person waking up to the delicious aromas of bread baking would use a logical sequence of physical senses to follow the path of smell (aroma wafting in the air), and hearing (noise in the kitchen). She or he would walk to the kitchen connecting the sensory information that bread is baking in the oven. Then to conclude without a shadow of a doubt that bread is in the oven, he or she must see the bread baking. Once the person physically sees the evidence—the bread in the oven—this reinforces the belief that the physical senses will not steer him or her wrong.

How wonderful and safe this conditioning makes us feel. Intuition is not logical; thus, people often do not consider it safe because we are going against the conditioning of our physical senses. When you are claiming your light and working with the foundation and anchor point of the magnetic light grid (the topics of chapter 3), intuition is the natural extension of our true self of light. We naturally grow and expand every day with our physical form. Our cells dance and celebrate being part of the greater whole of our body. So, too, does our light dance and celebrate being part of the greater whole of all.

I have always known intuition was my birthright as a being of love and light. I was gifted with seeing the world as moving dots of vibrant color until I was three years old. After breaking my leg twice when I was three, I grasped the belief that the vivid colored dots I was seeing were dense forms, holding boundaries of pain, pleasure, and assured safety in my growth as a human being. By learning my lessons of condition well, it took a three-dimensional experience with an Angel to crack my conditioning so I could return to naturally seeing my landscape as vibrant colors. Now living my life fully in co-creation with my intuition, joy is my expression. For, intuition is being in tune with the highest aspect of me.

Life is joy. Intuition is your perfect connection to all that you are. At first, your intuition may feel random, and you will question the insight you receive from it. Yet, that hunch, that gut feeling, or that knowingness represents that you are in tune to the fullest expression of your light. The gift of co-creating with your intuition is knowing without a shadow of a doubt who you are and how you can truly be purposeful while experiencing the landscape around you. You are looking at the gift of "as above, so below," or of what you know as yourself above now being brought to you here, and "as within, so without," so that you can take actions outward based on what you know without a doubt.

Intuition builds that GPS unit within your heart. I call it my GPU—God-positioning unit—because I know with certainty that each step I take is what I am supposed to be doing. Sometimes it looks out of order, or without definition, but because I know my light and my love, I am following my truth.

We have all had an experience involving intuition. A common occurrence is to think of someone we have not seen or heard from in a while and then shortly afterward, out of nowhere, this person shows up in our lives. We dream while sleeping, and many of us, shortly after waking, find ourselves in the same specific situations in our waking reality. As you begin to rely on the unified aspect and become more receptive to information received intuitively, you will advance mentally, emotionally, and spiritually at a much faster rate compared to individuals who limits themselves to just the information they obtain from their five senses.

We all have random experiences of intuition, but to actually induce this type of experience, and to call forth this higher level of intelligence at will, takes practice for all of us. One of the most effective paths is to just have fun co-creating with your intuition.

The Imagined House

By exercising your imagination and expanding your physical senses, you have time to play with your mind's eye to gain experience receiving answers from you. It also contains elements similar to dream interpretation.

Your house often is a symbol of yourself, your own personality. In this exercise, you will explore a mental imagery scene of a house. Afterward, consider what the various characteristics of the house may say something about your personality. Pay attention to such details as how the house appears on the inside as opposed to the outside, what can and cannot be found inside the house, how you enter the house, what is inside the "secret" room, colors, textures, how space is experienced, and so on. All of these details may have symbolic significance. You may be amazed by what the imagined house says about you.

The Imagined House Meditation

Find a comfortable place to sit or lie down, and follow these directions. You are walking down a road, and you see a house. What details jump out at you? What is your first impression?

Continue walking up to the house. How do you feel? You see a path that takes you around that house. Take that path and notice the details of the whole house as you walk around it. Now come back to the front of that house.

Walk up to the front door and enter the house. What do you see? Explore the house. Check out the different rooms and note what is in them. Take time to explore.

When you are ready, you find a secret door that leads to a secret room. Go inside that room. Focus on the details. Find pieces of you that you have tucked away in this room. This safe space holds all the secrets of you. When you are ready, leave the secret room.

Go back into the main part of the house. Notice any details that you missed the first time through. Leave the house through the front door. As you walk away, turn back and look at the house one more time. Turn and walk down the road away from the house and continue walking.

When you are ready, leave this scene, bringing with you your remembrances of the house. Each piece of this house holds a connection to you. Take time to contemplate the meaning of the details, and to fully connect back to you. If you are in a group setting, compare what you saw with others and talk about the meaning of what you saw.

Mental Attunement

Mental attunement is the main thing that a person has to be able to grasp and hold when it comes to entering into the

24

arena of doing energy or intuition work. Energy flows not only through your body but also through all aspects of your mind all the time. So, to do really good energy work, you have to have clarity of your mind which can be attained through mental attunement and meditation. Being disorganized is not helpful in energy work.

Consider my story. When the Angel first appeared to me, I felt that perfect oneness, but my mind was so disorganized that I had only moments of true clarity. And so, as you have a clear mind and hold perfect love of the Divine, it becomes the universal chemical for all healings. To have Divine Love come through, you need to have an open mind for it to filter through. Everyday things, such as life, family, and work, can interfere with maintaining a clear mind, which is why prayer and meditation are so important.

As you work on clearing your mind, you will be able to hold that clarity longer and longer. You will get better at it, and eventually, you will able to get into clarity instantly. One book I highly recommend is *The Lightworker's Way* by Doreen Virtue. In this book, she talks about mental attunement, identifying yourself with Absolute Love, and really sitting with meditation and clearing yourself. Your job is always and only to heal yourself. You are never healing anyone else because you are always whole.

In duality, when you radiate back that wholeness, you add the Absolute Love that you are trying to remember. So, although we are serving others, we are also serving ourselves by being one in remembering love. That is why you "do unto others as you would do unto yourself." It is all about you. This game of life is built all around you. Everything in your awareness is all about you. We have a large gray zone in our minds, yet it is always connected to our conscious mind and superconscious mind. We have to clear those waters. You have to get dirty and live through some difficult experiences because you can only look at yourself in this way.

Remember that you can release your contract of whatever is causing the trouble in your life and say, "I will be fully present, do the best I can, and get better every day in every way." In the metaphysical world, the term for the superconsciousness is Higher Self. When we ask for information and really live in that divine space, we are in our Higher Self.

Intention

Without intention there is not progression.
Create the peace,
create the love,
create the fog
by intention.
Done correctly you will have what you want.
Intention is so simple.
Create the thought,
flow it to your heart,
believe in its life,
and you will have mastered what brought you here.
Intention will only work if it is the truth.
God will help you control your desire.
Listen to him and be what you have always wanted to be.

~ Mike Russell

Chapter 3

Claiming Your Light and
the Magnetic Light Grid

*Knowledge seekers want to know a specific way
that they can connect to Source, and they know
that this connection has to be made.*

Claiming Your Light is a healing practice given to me by
Archangel Raphael that actively forgives our split mind,
which holds judgments and helps the pain and pleasure
stories to disappear into the eternal wholeness of Spirit.

To connect the dots in using Claim Your Light healing
practice, the Spirit, the ego, and the soul need to be defined.
The Spirit refers to our essence, which is whole and innocent
in oneness with our creator, Absolute Love. Your Spirit never
leaves you. The ego is the energy of duality that the split
mind holds of physical reality. The soul is the essence of our
energy that binds our alpha, or beginning in duality, to our
omega, or ending in duality. The core essences of the soul
are light and love. Its energy contains all the pieces of your
past lives, personality, temperament, and emotional triggers
that allow you to see, feel, hear, and know Absolute Love in
every particle of duality. In each incarnation, your soul
comes with all the remembrances of how you love and how
you are to love.

Archangel Raphael showed me that the soul is like a fruit
salad. Each person brings all different flavors and textures
that create the sweet and sour of the person before you.
When you claim your light, you pick one event, or one piece

29

of fruit, to chew deeply on, questioning how to fully digest the substance of that event to bring understanding and forgiveness in love and light to your mind, heart, and soul.

This healing practice brings back all the energy you have given to past experiences that you hold onto in pain and fear. By claiming your light, you are bringing the energy—the sour pieces of fruit—that feeds your ego and holds us captive in your duality. By bringing that energy back to the core essence of your soul, through love, you claim your light in who you are as a holy temple: your physical body.

When you actively claim your core truths of love and light, your soul will align events and/or people from this lifetime or from previous life times, to reclaiming the light of your energy that is stuck in pain, suffering, or any place you felt a lack of love. Your energy—your soul—is constant. Taking back negative energy and infusing this energy with light enliven your expression of joy and, consequently, love. For me, by claiming my light at each moment, I actively create my full force of light and love, bringing everyday experiences into the perfection of who I am.

When stressed, pained, and fearful, the conscious, or split mind builds an energy bubble of worry and anxiety that is so strong it must explode outward to find release. Once it does, instead of being a unified force centered in your core of love and light, your energy is scattered into a million particles. The more particles your essence becomes, the less effective you can be in bringing your truth to your environment. The moment your energy bubble explodes, your Guardian Angels hug that energy field so that when we are ready to retrieve those particles, they can be united in the essence of love, holding the perfection that you are.

We run from our light and the source of pain because we believe there is more fear and punishment. The greatest gift is that our Angel is hugging us and if we just turn around into the essence of Spirit, we can see that all is well. If you call in that pain and sit with it, you will recognize that there is no fear or punishment. It is just an event and you are facing it.

Our Spirit is truly our light, just as our deepest joy and deepest fear are our light. In that place of duality, just seeing that our light is our greatest gift can bring deep peace. Once you stop fighting it, your life reality truly helps you to be that whole person in what you want to accomplish in your light and what you came here for.

The Gift of Claiming Your Light

Because you are whole and not of a split mind, you do not have any divided forces within your energy field. When we claimed our light, we brought back pieces of lost energy to remember our wholeness.

Claiming your light gives you the opportunity to look at the need or the trigger that is happening in your energy field at this moment and gives you the freedom to react differently. As Archangel Raphael says, "in the power of three, times three, times three, you know thee." You know who you are, so you can be in that full conscious placement of movement forward of who you truly are. You might really want that doughnut you are craving, but know that your want is perfect and that there is no judgment on it. It is not good or bad; it is just what you need. Give yourself the space to understand the whole knowledge of why and then claim happiness and that you are choosing to claim it. My Spirit is happy, and the gift is being whole and happy in love and joy and of having peace. By claiming your light, you are choosing to create with your light and to know your goodness.

With the gift and anchor of Archangel Raphael, I was ready to claim my light regarding my posttraumatic stress from going to the dentist. I had a toothache that was getting worse and worse. No matter the level of my pain, I procrastinated in calling the dentist. Finally, the pain kept me up all night, and I realized I was creating pure madness in my life. I heard Archangel Raphael say that the only way for me to stop the madness now and forever was to claim my light, and thus my power to get my tooth fixed.

So after numbing my mouth, I sat on my porch and visualized Archangel Raphael hugging me. As I took a deep breath and allowed his essence to flow through me, I felt my throat getting cold. I saw the dentist yelling at me when I was five. I could not sit still; I squirmed and tried to relax in a dentist chair that was way too big for my small body. His voice was projected at my throat. His strong, hard voice overwhelmed me.

As I released my breath, I saw that my dentist was frustrated because his talent was not working with little kids. I saw the scratches in my cells begin to heal as I brought light to the fact that my dentist had been doing his best with what he had to work with at the time. This light healed my cells of this traumatic memory, allowing all my cells shine more clearly.

With my next deep breath, I instantly felt my gut tighten with fear. My heart pounded louder and louder. I was moved to moan until the pain in my gut resonated with that tone. Soon my moan turned into laughter, joy ringing through my throat. I felt powerful in expressing my needs especially in a dental environment.

Finally, I took in one more deep breath seeing my energy one with Archangel Raphael's essence. I shouted, "I am light; I am one in Absolute Love." I knew I had healed my posttraumatic stress concerning the dentist. I got up and made the appointment to get my tooth fixed.

Yes! Claim your light and feel the full power of you.

How to Claim Your Light

To claim your light, first you must stop running, giving into the flight of your fight-or-flight reflex, from the memory of the experience that needs to be healed. Be still, as still as your mind will allow. Visualize your Guardian Angel, or any Angelic presence, hugging you in his or her Holy essence.

Now breathe deeply the loving essence from your Angel. Become aware of how your body responds to the energy of the memory of the situation you are healing. Be mindful of any hot spots, cold spots, and painful spots on your body. These represent places you have unconsciously stored the cellular memory of this event.

Release your breath while visualizing the light of you energized with the Angel's presence. Shatter the dark spots in your cells, release the physical memory, and bring that cell back to your light.

Again, breathe deeply, taking in the loving essence from your Angel. This time, be aware of how you react to the emotional cues of this experience. Are you sweating? Is your heart pounding? Does your stomach ache? These feelings are valid; having them is neither good nor bad, but they are valid.

Move with your emotions: yell, cry, laugh, and/or moan until you can express no more. As you move through your emotions, your light will replace any clouds of heaviness this experience triggered. Breathe until you feel the joy of breathing light into and out of your body. You have expanded your energy field to the highest vibration of you.

Now once again breathe deeply the loving essence of your Angel. You and Your Guardian Angel are one, erasing from your Alpha and Omega the core negative energy that is triggering your darkness. Exclaim in your mind, heart, and soul, "I am light; I am one in Absolute Love."

The Magnetic Light Grid

Everything in the universe communicates through light via the magnetic light grid. We have forgotten over time that this is the most natural, truest way to communicate with everything around us, including other people, animals, plants and every particle of our landscape through the communication system call the magnetic light grid. The gift of the Holy Spirit is to hold the magnetic light grid in Absolute Love so that we can find our way out of this illusion through the light of us. A goal we have in every lifetime is to strengthen our light, thus enhancing our connection with the magnetic light grid.

The more we connect to the magnetic light grid, the deeper and clearer we are in tune with the essence of the Holy Spirit. This is when your intuition becomes an extension of the physical senses with your physical form. You truly are the holy temple of light and love.

When you claim your light, you will feel a heightened and stronger energy field around you because your light is energizing the particles of all of you. Because we have duality, we have positive and negative poles of energy flowing within our energy field. The more we claim our light, and the stronger our field resonates in light, the easier holding your focus and clarity with others, the Holy Spirit, and all realms of being will be. Your light will be able to attract and connect with others near or far. You become the beacon, serving others in their quest in claiming their light.

When you first reach inward and outward along the magnetic light grid, you might suffer some physical discomforts like headaches, earaches, dizziness, and flu-like symptoms. Do not worry. You are being hugged by your Guardian Angel. Your light and your Angel's essence are the best prescription for whole health. Remember to claim your light and surrender to the comfort of your Angel's hugs.

Although the magnetic light grid has always been there, when you develop oneness with it, the grid will seem like a whole new system. As a beginner, you may see a blank field or area with flashes. As you meditate and the light communicates, you will see the energy of the white light becoming stronger and more fluid. It may look like clouds. Mine is like SOS energy: flashing of lights of different intensities, as if a message is being sent. It filters into my mind and creates pictures or words that I say aloud.

You will build these images with experience. At first, many people only see flashes of white within the field, which eventually develop into more pronounced visual patterns. Because you are building these images, they will eventually become three-dimensional and appear in your space. So when you start resonating in this way, you are training your mind so that your body's eyes can see this energy in its three-dimensional form.

Then you can be in tune with all light energy. You can pick up on global events also. For instance, you might feel energy in your third eye and later discover that an earthquake occurred somewhere. Picking up on these things will become easy because we are all one and we are all connected in light through the magnetic light grid. Each light that you see in the grid is a person, an event, or a thought that you can call to you. You can think of it as similar to your body: every cell in your body is separate, but it is also a part of, and in constant communication with, the whole.

The gifts we receive when we claim our light and connect to the magnetic light grid allow the Angels to raise our vibration to meet and more closely match the vibration of the Guides we want to call in.

As you meditate and get your vibration going, you are also allowing that part of you that is your personality to step out of your body, and be the Spirit you are. Once you break through any wall that you have within your third eye and fully connect to the magnetic light grid, you will become one with all particles of the universe.

How to Connect to the Magnetic Light Grid

Your light and your Angel's essence are the best prescription for your complete health. Remember to claim your light and surrender to the comfort of your Angel's hugs. Once you learn what light feels like, the more you can connect to it intentionally, instead of accidentally.

Now you are ready to connect with the magnetic light grid with clear intention for the highest and best. One of my favorite ways to purposefully build my connection with the magnetic light grid is through The Pink Light Meditation. What I like about this meditation is that it helps focus the mind so it can become involved in the process. You activate the cells in your mind and remember your connection to the magnetic grid, which is connected with the earth and with all the forces around us. The more you do this meditation, the more you will be able to send and receive information and to intentionally be in tune with the magnetic light grid rather than having the impression that everything is an accident. This is the same process for telepathy and automatic writing. This meditation helps you to remember the bone-basic way to connect. You are bringing oneness to the left and right hemispheres of your brain, and when they work together, you invoke the cells of the mind and hone it through the third eye. Read it, try it, and enjoy the full energy experience of this meditation.

The Pink Light Meditation

Sit comfortably and relax into the chair, allowing all your worries about life to dissipate. Visualize a beautiful ball of gold energy coming down from heaven. It comes down through the top of your head, and down through your spinal column. The energy runs deep down into the core of Mother Earth. As this energy of light comes through you, it brings the energy of Divine Light back to our conscious awareness and to the conscious memory in the cells. Notice that golden energy raining down roots into Mother Earth and anchoring the joy of sharing as above, so below.

From the core of Mother Earth, see the silver ray of Divine receptivity. Allow the silver ray to come up through your feet and knees, through your hips and spinal column to the top of your head, before sprinkling all around you as a fountain of youth and vitality that enters all the cells, thoughts, and the aura field. Release again all your worries and concerns and connect to the highest truth, remembering that everything is one in Divine Love.

Now with intention and focus, create a ball of pink energy right behind your forehead. See this energy field heal your split mind, forming a singular focus. See the energy field bridge the right and left hemispheres, connecting the activity to your eyes. Open your energy field to the pink light of love and compassion and see how this ball of energy feels to you in your mind's eye. Bring the energy ball in your head to just an inch outside of your head and watch it fill the space and take up an inch around your entire body. Allow this beautiful pink Divine Light and Love soak into your body. Note how this energy feels around you.

Now, push the energy out about five feet from your body. Direct that energy field to fill the space with this pink light. Any earthly concerns—money, friends, work—can be left outside the pink light. For now, you are holding the magnetic light grid that can interface with the Divine Light and Love. You can also create a purpose for how your unlimited supply of stress can be released.

As you do this, consider how it feels to be embraced in the pink light of Divine Love. Now, allow the energy of who you really are to expand as large as you are comfortable with, connecting it to all who are part of you and knowing that you are fully protected in this Divine bubble of love. Look back at your body and see how truly you are protected within the one-inch to five-foot bubble you have created. Feel the pulse of the family of humankind that you are one with. Also, feel the pulse of the trees, the animals, the minerals, and all the Spirit Guides and Angels. We are all one.

What you are doing at this point is creating the pathways for your highest mind to register the patterns of all light that extend forever in celebration of creation in your DNA field. Everyone has the ability to channel and to participate in a Divine connection of the oneness.

Now, as you pull your energy back to your body, give gratitude and thanks. Bring your energy to within one inch of your body. Feel the changes within the energy. Is the vibration around you a little more buoyant and buzzy?

Focus the ball of energy at the center of your mind. Notice how your head, your body's eyes, and the cells around those eyes feel. Are they warm or tingling? They are destined for a purpose. Now, as you stay connected to the earth, come back to feeling your body. When you are ready to open your eyes, do so. You are one in light, and you are one in Absolute Love.

The Expanded Pink Light Meditation

This expanded version of the pink light meditation allows you to tune in deeper to the magnetic light grid.

Get comfortable and relax. Repeat the same process of meditation you performed in the pink light meditation. Once you take the pink light out five feet through your auric field, visualize it also clearing your physical body of any energy that would burden the expression of oneness. Release all fear, all feelings of lack, and all limitations. Visualize the forehead area in the shape of a cone that gets larger as it moves away from you. It goes all the way out to five feet. Once you see the cone, remember how it feels and how it looks. At the larger end of the cone is a brick wall. In your mind's eye, travel to the larger end and look at your brick wall. Note what it feels like: what is the texture and how high it is. As you look it over, find the weakest point on your brick wall. Now, with your visual body, push the brick wall down. If the brick wall does not come down, try sending energy from your hand to the weakest point on the wall. Keep sending energy until the brick wall comes down.

Behind the wall is the magnetic light grid. It might be a black void with little white flashes flying around in it. When you see the magnetic light grid, say your name aloud three times. Now look to see if one of the flashes responds back to you. Are you picking up on any sound or visions? Are any impressions being put into your mind? Does your mind's eye feel different? Now, ask to communicate with somebody, and then ask a question and note any responses.

When you finish sharing information, give thanks and gratitude and come back to your body while staying aware of the warmth that you are. What that phase did was set your body up for the understanding of light and remembering how to communicate with it.

An Additional Meditation

The following meditation is another you can use to claim your light.

Sit comfortably with your feet on the floor and your hands in your lap. Take three deep cleansing breaths, bringing the air in through the nose and out through your mouth. On the third exhale, imagine roots growing from the bottom of your feet down through the floor and into the ground, connecting you securely to earth. With your next exhale, imagine a ball of beautiful healing white light just above your head. As you breathe, imagine this light slowly descending around you and encompassing your head, shoulders, torso, hips, legs, and feet. You are now surrounded by the white light of love and protection. You are safe, secure, protected, and loved.

During your next exhale, imagine a beam of white light rising from the top of your head and reaching up into the sky—up, up, up to the universe beyond. Now you are in the presence of pure light energy. All that we ever are is part of this pure white energy. You are in peace, and when you are ready, ask the Angels to raise your vibration to more closely fit the vibration of your Divine blueprint to manifest into form. Remember this vibration and impress it into your mind, body, and cells. You now are fully creating your life in the highest purpose of you.

You are ready to fully express your intuition in every movement of your life. You are in the perfect dance with the Holy Spirit. When you are ready, take a deep breath and return to the feelings of your body. Stay relaxed as you fully become present in all your senses.

Ancient Gift

Ancient art of energy work,
concentrated into the flow of power,
healing beyond the human senses,
sends its message to the body.
Belief in the help,
is not a requirement.
Feeling the relief is the gift.
Learning the abundance
of the universal life force, opens the mind,
to free the Spirit and focus the energy
where it needs to go.
Hold onto the thought,
that we can all be healed,
and rejoice in the love that the energy brings.

~ Mike Russell

Chapter 4

Spiritual Protection and Grounding

*Knowledge seekers want to know
that while they are developing skills within
the spiritual venue, they will
be safe during the journey.*

Protection and grounding are important to you if you believe that you can be affected by different negative energies. Setting the stage to protect and ground yourself is a good habit to get into not only for you as an individual but also for the space you use until you have progressed to a higher level of energy and no longer need them.

Protection

To me, there are many schools of thought focused on psychic and spiritual protection. The most important point to remember is that these techniques are remedial in that they are only necessary as long as you believe or give power to lower-vibration energies. There are actually no dark forces per se, only energies and entities that have very little light or love. Protection techniques are designed to withdraw energies from the illusion of darkness. Once a soul rises to a level of love, spiritual protection is no longer necessary.

There are two approaches to spiritual protection: embracing the light and dispelling the darkness. When releasing energies, entities, or thought forms, you always visualize them moving into the light of Divine Love with your blessings and with a sense of well-being. Releasing anything in anger does not dispel it because the vibration of anger is what attracts such energies in the first place. So forgiveness is essential if you want to live a life free of energetic attachments.

Many people who come to me want to know how I have protected the healing room I work out of. I always tell them that I seal this room in the white light of Divine Love. I can run energy lines around each corner of the room. Some people even like to participate in a ritual with me to know that they are safe. My pure intent is to provide that safe place for them. I sometimes call in the prayer of protection using Divine Love. It is all about their need at the time.

I know that I am Divine Love, and so in that belief, I am totally protected. I am not being attacked from anything because in Divine Love, all is perfect. The reason that I discuss protection is that most people have a preconceived notion that they have to be protected from evil. So by learning proper grounding and protection techniques, they can cancel any negative forces that they have around them that is part of their pain story.

I see Divine Love as insulation around a cord that runs from Source to something. Divine Love insulates everything. When you have that insulation around your energetic connection, you can pick up a wire and be safe while conducting a great amount of energy. If someone does believe in dark forces, then it is that reminder that light always wins out over darkness. When you have a little candle and you show them that it brightens the whole room, they feel safe.

Because I was brought up in the Catholic Church, I am very aware of the concept of good and evil. When I first started doing psychic and spiritual work, I thought I needed some type of sword and shield to protect myself. Quickly I realized that if I am always protecting myself with an image of a hard object like my shield, I am not receiving all my client's information and Divine Love. I was blocking my gifts and resisting the flow of Divine Love because of this fear. In Divine Love, there is no resistance, so I had to change my paradigm, too, and know that Divine Love is everywhere and everything.

When I have a client on the healing table or when I am doing a psychic reading, and I feel a dark force around us, I instantly call on our Guardian Angels to hug us in their wings, which creates a tube of Divine Love. Next, I visualize the light of Divine Love slowly illuminating the dark force, glowing the way to heaven. If the dark energy persists, I ask that energy, "Are you of love and light?" three times. If the energy is not here for the highest and best purpose, the Angels of Light will escort it out.

Your Guardian Angel is always your best protection against all dark forces. Release all darkness in love and light, and you will receive your highest and best. As you are working, your connection gets deeper and clearer to Divine Love. There is no way you can be attacked and lose your free will to darkness. People have all spectrums of light and dark forces around them. When you sit across from another, you might work with the good, the bad, or both. Darkness is the lack of light. As your light shines, the darkness will be released forever in that light. What a great gift of shining your light and dissolving the darkness forever. We fear what we do not know. Once you shine your light on darkness, you know it was just the lack of light. Yes, light always wins over darkness. For light is the higher vibration of existence.

After the Angel visited me, many energy forms would visit me especially at night. I would wake from a deep sleep and feel a presence. I would throw a blanket over my head and ask, "Are you of Love and Light?" three times. As given to me by the Angelic realm, if you ask an energy three times, it must answer yes or no. If the answer is yes, then you can make friends. If the answer is no, the Angels of Light escort them away. For me, I heard the answer, "Yes, Trisha." Thus, protection and grounding will put you in the right place mentally, emotionally, and physically for you to not engage in other people's stories.

Protection Techniques

The following techniques can be done for protection. They provide ways for you to feel comfortable and protected.

Declaring Your Sovereignty

You can issue the following command, repeating it until you feel complete. For example,

"I am of love and light. I command all energies, entities and thought forms that are not whole in Absolute Love to leave my space now and forever. I am of love and light."

Then picture the forms leaving and drifting up into the light of God. Then say,

"I forgive you, release you and bless you to go to your highest and best."

Replacing Your Guides

Visualize your Guides if you can and say, "At this time, all Beings of Absolute Love who are aligned with me, surround me and participate in my journey. See the Guides that are not whole in Absolute Love, drifting into the light."

Say, "Thank you for your service. I bless you and wish you well in your journey to light."

Visualize new Guides descending into your space. Welcome them and thank them for their upcoming service to the light. Another technique that you can do when you are driving or busy and cannot take time to meditate is chanting aloud or silently. You can say,

I am light and love.
I am light and love.
I am light and love.

Grounding

Beyond spiritual protection, being grounded is very important. One substantial thing that you need to do when working with energy and helping others heal or when facilitating some form of healing or reading is to find ways to ground yourself.

Grounding connects your energy to the earth in a stable, secure way. It allows you to rid yourself of unwanted energy and to take in clean, balanced energy. When you are well grounded, drawing energy through yourself is much easier. For me, grounding is just making things stable. It helps me feel whole in my body. When you are grounded, you can then feel connected to the earth's energy and hold it in an unwavering, sustainable field. What can happen if you do not ground yourself as a healer or reader is that you can get migraines or become dizzy. You can also feel like you are going crazy because of the thoughts or energy coming and going. This practice is great for feeling strong within your own energy field that you are building.

Be mindful of all ways you are connecting to your body, connecting to the earth, connecting to others, and connecting to Divine Love. Wake up each morning aware of connecting to your now. For me, with each sip of my morning coffee, I see my body waking up, connecting to each cell, connecting to my environment, connecting to my family, and connecting to Mother Earth, Father Sky, and Divine Love. Each sip awakens my connections and deep gratitude for my life. As I become anchored in my body, my breathing, and my mind, I am grounded in the motion of my day. Many times, I see some people's energy wildly spinning in their bodies, their emotions, their thoughts, and their environments.

Grounding is pivotal in building a stable, safe structure for thriving in life. There are many ways to ground. All attentive exercises of mind, emotion, body, and energy that connect you deeply to Mother Earth and to all particles in the environment around you are perfect. A mindful walking meditation is great for connecting on all levels. Another technique is to visualize roots growing from your feet and going deep into Mother Earth. As you connect, feel the love and light energy that Mother Earth is constantly sending to us to grow and thrive on her surface. Using stones and crystals is a fun way to ground yourself and to feel your connection to Mother Earth's gifts. Eating organic fruits and vegetables connect your cells to the cells of Mother Earth's abundances and harvest. Wow, how lucky are we to give and receive the blessings our landscape holds.

Another benefit is that the more grounded you are, the less you are to become attached to other people's stories of pain. You can be only a witness offering a safe, secure place for inviting a new perspective and for changing the pain to understanding of separation and healing back to Oneness. When I am perfectly grounded, I can hold a safe, secure space, giving a clean, clear structure to be a witness to another's pain story without taking it on. I hug us in the wings of our Guardian Angels allowing Divine Love to heal all. Showing up and being able to be present are huge blessings. That is why grounding is so important.

Grounding also provides protection from the ego-consciousness. I know that if I am grounded within myself and in all my connections and that I am hugged in Divine Love, I will experience no backlash. If something triggers me into negative thinking, then I know I have healing in myself to attend to.

During a healing or reading, I sit in the director's chair, get part of the script, and watch it play out. Everyone who comes into my healing space is different and comes with his or her own story, or alpha and omega. An analogy is that each person brings in his or her own deck of cards and plays a different game with those cards. Because of this, each person shows the cards that he or she needs to show me. But I do not know what other cards are in the person's hand. That is not up to me to know anyway. But throughout the healing or psychic session, if the Divine Force wants those cards to be revealed, they are. Each game is different. Some people play blackjack, wanting you to have a certain card. Some people play rummy or some other game. It is OK because I love them and it is what is needed. Each card could represent a relationship, a financial issue, or something tied to work. When the person is sitting there, I am seeing the cards they are holding at the time. I am just a witness.

Whatever a person's alpha-and-omega story line shows is what the Angels know, and I walk away from each healing session in awe because of this. As a person's cards are laid down in their time, it is all perfect. The client typically is not grounded, which is why you provide the perfect conduit, something for them to sink into. That is why he or she has come to you anyway. What he or she wants is to have some peace somewhere, which includes peace of mind, emotion, and body.

One way I test how grounded I am is to go to a playground, get on the seesaw, and see how long I can keep it balanced. It really does provide a good visual. I then know what it feels like so before a session I can hold that energy field and no one is going to pull me off balance. Healers are the same as everyone else in that they can have off-balance days during which they are not grounded properly.

When I am grounded, I feel as though I have a certain rhythm. When I am unbalanced, everything is out of sync, and I catch on to it quickly. I feel like I am playing jazz in a classical music event. My energy is improvising when it should be flowing in a more direct manner. It is pretty obvious, and I will go outside and walk barefooted in the grass to anchor myself to the earth; then a calmness comes over me.

Grounding activities vary from person to person—some people drink coffee, hug a tree, carry obsidian or hematite stone, jog, or do some other type of physical activity—but everyone experiences signs that their energy level has changed, meaning that it is time to ground yourself. Some of these signs include

- ✓ feeling out of balance because of the new energy you are receiving;
- ✓ feeling that you cannot release an energy that is bothering you;
- ✓ feeling overwhelming sadness, anger, or old emotions that you are having a hard time releasing; and
- ✓ feeling of negative energy around or within you.

Be mindful of how you interact with yourself, with others, and with your environment, and you will notice whether you are grounded or not. You are the key in perfecting this simple act of participating fully in life.

The Path

Connect the dots
along the way,
seeing people
for the first time or last.
Watch the signs
and reflect on the connection
that bring the daily miracles
into your worldly focus.
Choose to react
or merely watch it happen.
Being open to the possibilities
will send light to your soul.

~ Mike Russell

Chapter 5

The Spiritual Body and the Chakras

*Knowledge seekers constantly search for
definitions and meaning to the things that they
cannot see, feel, hear, and know to explain
their universe better.*

The Supple Body

All the layers of your energy fields affect the wholeness of you
(see figure 1). Being aware of each layer of your energy body
that extends from your physical body allows you to fully own
that you are the creator of all your experiences and that you
are in complete control of receiving your highest and best.

The etheric energy body is close, within two inches, to the
physical body. It is like having a body double that contains
all the structures in the body. It reflects what the body is
experiencing. Any problems with the physical body will show
up as a weak area in the etheric field, which sometimes
manifests itself as a hot or cold spot. A strong physical body
makes for a strong first auric layer. Being mindful of your
physical body, you become mindful of the etheric energy
field.

The emotional energy body is the field in which emotional
energy flows; it extends out to three inches from the body.
Colors are the indicators of this field. Emotions and feelings
create the spectrum of color. For example, bright colors
indicate happy uplifting emotions, and muddy colors indicate
negative feelings toward yourself or others. When people are

not allowed to express their emotions and feelings, damage occurs in this energy field. The unexpressed emotions hinder the flow of energy ultimately disrupting the other energy layers and creating disease in the physical body.

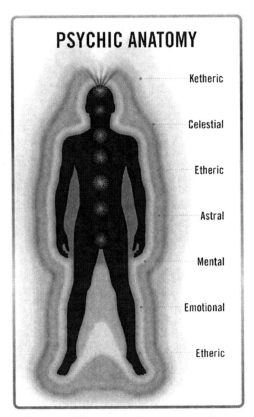

PSYCHIC ANATOMY

Ketheric

Celestial

Etheric

Astral

Mental

Emotional

Etheric

Figure 1: The Basic Psychic Anatomy

The mental energy body is the field in which mental energy flows and extends from three to eight inches. Our thoughts create this field's vibrancy. Happy, loving thoughts add a vibrant high frequency to this field. Negative talk deadens this field, closing the ease of connecting with the rational and intuitive sides of a person's mind. With negative thoughts, this layer flows very slowly, causing distortion in reality.

The astral energy body is a person's connection to others and his or her environment. It extends out about a foot. A strong, healthy field has an easy energy flow. It pulsates out to all connections around them. An unhealthy field will seem sticky, dark, and mucus-like. Tuning into this field, you are able to get a basic understanding of a person's overall health in relationships.

The etheric field is the field of Divine Will. It looks like a halo surrounding all the other energy fields. Your life patterns and life destinies are created and manifested here. This field is where you as a soul have the divine will to either align with the pattern of universal purpose or not. But those who do will feel a sense of connectedness to the universe and their life purpose. Their life has order. If this field is weak or distorted, the person will feel a need to be righteous in their own life patterns seeking their own will be done no matter the cost.

The celestial energy body is composed of beautiful, shimmering light radiating out in all directions. An unstructured field of very high-frequency energy, it is associated with the more spiritual emotional states of unconditional love and joy and is the level of Divine Love and spiritual feelings. A healthy sixth auric level appears bright and highly charged. The key to having more spiritual experiences is charging this auric level by focusing your mind on meditative practices.

The ketheric field reflects the Divine Mind. When healthy, it looks like beautiful golden lines of high-frequency energy, which are very, very strong. This energy extends outward from the body at a distance of about three feet, which is far enough from the body to appear to be hugging the person, holding them in an egg-shaped energy field.

When this layer is healthy, the subject feels a conscious awareness of the Divine Mind field and the great universal interconnectedness. Creativity will abound, and the person will be able to understand the broad, overall concepts about the nature of existence and Divine Truth. An unhealthy field often appears dull, weak, and thinner in some areas than others. It may even be torn, allowing energy to leak from the subject's aura. The person with an unhealthy ketheric field may feel isolated from the Divine and any universal truths about creation and divinity.

An Energy Exercise

Pair up with someone. Place your hands three inches above the open palms of another person. Feel the energy coming off each other. Then move your hands farther apart and see how far away your hands can be from the other person and still feel the energy between you.

If you are by yourself, you can use other items, such as a plant or a piece of fruit, or you can work with your own body. Clap your hands together to energize them and try to feel the energy from various things. Take note of what you are feeling.

The Chakra System

The different energy fields around the body can be discussed in more detail by using the chakra system (see figure 2). The word chakra is Sanskrit for "wheel" or "disk" and signifies one of seven major energy centers in the body. Each chakra correlates to a specific region within your physical body. For example, the heart chakra encompasses the heart, lungs, rig cage, and all the systems within that area.

Seven basic chakras overlay the physical body. There are many more chakras, but we focus on the seven basic chakras. As dimensional vortices within the supple and physical body, chakras take in and process high vibrational energies. It is almost like sifting flour. Energy is sifted through these different levels. The study of the major chakras would be the key. Because they are connected to the supple body, you have the opportunity to respond through the physical, mental, and emotional fields at each level. The chakra system can be read about in greater detail as a number of books are available on the subject.

Here, I want to cover the basics of each chakra as it fits nicely into our discussion on energy (see table 1). So, as we balance the chakras and clean them, it allows us to feel more of our self-definition, self-acceptance, self-expression, self-reflection, and self-knowledge.

In addition, through our exercises in forgiveness the chakra system is affected because we are learning to hold a unified and balanced field around each chakra. A unified and balanced field is a perfect field. The more balanced you are, the more balanced you are in your self-awareness, self-reflection, and self-identity and the more you hold your core truths, the more you are in the Divine placement of perfection.

When we hold the knowledge of who we truly are, which is the holy presence and the holy power of Absolute Love, and the oneness of Divine Love, then we can project that clearly to others without having any expectations or motivations. Clearing and balancing are really good exercises because you are building and clarifying the energy around you while meditating with Divine Love. You hold more and more energy through an attunement and become aware of a healthy chakra and how it feels within your energy field. It anchors you to keep going forward.

Once you get going, what is wonderful about energy is that it is Divine Intelligence energy, and it knows your perfect harmony in your energy field. You do not need to keep reminding your body every day to harmonize and balance. You can just visualize the colors of each chakra and "so be it." Your energy is balanced and harmonized.

Another thing I like to do when I feel out of balance is buy a bag of Skittles. They come in all colors and remind me of the rainbow. This allows me to see the chakras and have a hands-on balancing method. It reminds me internally of the fun that we are supposed to be having in sharing with Spirit. Chakras share energy with the body, but like when you throw a pebble in a pond, their energy ripples. So, for instance, the heart chakra ripples throughout your body. But, its focus is concentrated at the heart. It is the same for the other chakras. Each chakra shares energy with the others. If you go to the same pond and throw seven stones, you would see how those ripples interact with each other. When you are in good health, your chakras are all very clear and sparkle. You can have holy moments when the chakras are perfect, but usually one overrides the others.

As a beginner, you want your chakras to be about the same size. They should be about three to four inches in size. Because the chakras move, defining their shape is difficult. Many people think of them as cones as resembling colored water whirling down a drain, in that they are circles of energy swirling around vortex-like centers. The chakras appear from the front and the back of the body and do not always move in the same direction. Some people have chakras that run clockwise and others that run counterclockwise. All are different, and all have their own Divine purpose, which is perfect. When people come for healing because we are all unique and different, that is what makes it so addicting. They all present something unique even within the seven chakras.

Figure 2: The Basic Chakras

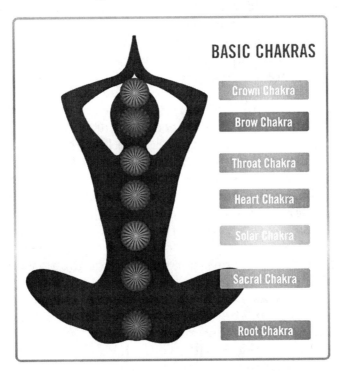

Table 1: The Chakras

Chakra	Color	Central Focus
1. Root Chakra	Red	The Physical Center; includes survival, and our connection to the earth that we live on
2. Sacral Chakra	Orange	The Emotional Center; includes creativity and sexuality
3. Solar Plexus Chakra	Yellow	The Personal Power Center; includes the ego emphasizing your will
4. Heart Chakra	Green	The Relationship Center; includes love, compassion and healing
5. Throat Chakra	Lt. Blue	The Communication Center; includes being creative and the way you self-express yourself
6. Third Eye or Brow Chakra	Dk. Blue	The Psychic Center; includes intuitive sight
7. Crown Chakra	Violet	The Spiritual Center; includes your connection to Spirit through self-knowledge

The Root Chakra

The first chakra is called the root chakra. Located at the base of the spine, it is about earth, physical identity, and orienting self-preservation and forms our foundation. It represents the element of earth and is, therefore, related to our survival instinct and to our sense of grounding and connection of our bodies to the physical plane. Ideally, this chakra brings up health, prosperity, security and dynamic presence. The color is red.

The Sacral Chakra

The sacral chakra, the second chakra, is located in the abdomen, the lower back, and the sexual organs. Related to the element of water and to emotions and sexuality, it connects us to others through our feelings, desires, sensations, and movements. Ideally, this chakra brings us fluidity and grace, sexual fulfillment, and the ability to accept change. Also, it brings emotional identity orientation. This is your creative center. It is orange in color.

The Solar Plexus Chakra

The third chakra is the solar plexus. This one is personal power identification, oriented to self-definition. This chakra is known as the power chakra, ruling our personal power, will, and autonomy. When healthy, this chakra brings us energy, effectiveness, spontaneity, and nondominating power. The color is yellow.

The Heart Chakra

The heart chakra is the chakra of a social identity and an indicator of self-acceptance. It is related to love and integrates the opposites in the psyche: mind and body, male and female, and duality and unity. A healthy fourth chakra allows us to love deeply, feel compassion, and have a deep sense of peace and centeredness. The color is green.

The Throat Chakra

The fifth chakra is centered on the throat. It is related to sound, communication, and self-expression as well as creativity. Through this chakra, we experience the world through the vibration of sound. The color is light blue.

The Third Eye Chakra

The third eye, or sixth chakra, is related to light identity with a focus on self-reflection. It is also known as the brow chakra. Related to the act of seeing both physically and intuitively, it opens our physic abilities. When it is healthy, it allows us to see clearly. In effect, it lets us see the big picture. The color is indigo or dark blue.

The Crown Chakra

The seventh chakra is called the crown chakra. It is related to thought, universal identity, and self-knowledge. Also, it is related to the consciousness of pure awareness. It is our connection to everything and everywhere. When developed, this chakra brings us knowledge, wisdom, understanding, and spiritual connection. The color is violet or purple.

The Hoop Chakra Demonstration

On the floor, lay out seven hoops, in the order of the chakras, to create a visualized spinal cord of a person. Similar to the chakras, which are always united and whirling together, the hoops should overlap to demonstrate how the chakras intermix their energies. No barriers separate the hoops (or chakras), for Spirit is always coloring outside any line of definition. Inside each hoop, place a colored ball that lights up in the corresponding hoop: red for the root charka, orange for the sacral chakra, and so on.

In your mind, build these fields of energy until you can see, feel, or sense the strength of the chakra color. The intensity of the colors will come and go because the chakras are constantly circulating. The energy is coming in to each chakra and circling out.

Reading Chakras

The base position, or that point closest to the physical body, of each chakra is more or less static along the grid of your spinal cord. This position collects all information moving through the chakras and then sends this information into each relating cell of your body. The energy pulsing through the chakras creates the energy that orbits through and around your body. Like a Hula-Hoop, your energy is always circulating and your field is always in motion.

When reading a person's energy field, keep in mind that chakras can be viewed from the front and the back of a body, concentrate on the base position of each chakra. The stronger the pulse of each base, the greater the light held and energizing the field. This pulse of light helps control the essence of the vibration of energy in and out with light energy. For a healthy body, you want the light in the chakras to pulse in time with your body's vibration. When you are clearing someone's chakra, you are mainly working within the base of each chakra's pivot point and the person's vibration.

The chakras are typically spinning inward toward the base position on the front of the body, in a clockwise direction and outward on the back of the body from the base position in a counterclockwise direction. There is no way of spinning that is technically correct. Which way the spin is only true for the person before you. Everybody's chakra system will spin differently.

When you start looking at a chakra system from a healing aspect, you are noticing the light of each chakra: How big is it? How open? Does the light pulsate and, if so, how? Sometimes you don't see any light, which indicates that the person is not comfortable in that chakra. Sometimes you see a great deal of light, which means that that person has a heightened importance of him-or herself in that chakra.

Our light has to fit our vibration to be truly the most authentic love for ourselves. Your core temperature is always changing, so your vibration is changing as well. When you try to assess these things, you may find it difficult to know whether you are looking at a very healthy system. One thing to consider is how much light there is coming from the person. If his or her body is well lit, then you know that the person is truly in his or her divine space, the space that he or she is meant to be in. Understanding a specific person's energy field and how his or her energy spins and swirls allows you to give a clearer reading. Remember, people's energy field can change over their lifetime.

Finding Cat Stevens

All my life, wondering through thought,
hoping to get a glimpse of the future.
Searching, seeking and finding everywhere
outside the master.
Going places I have never been,
asking questions to calm the din.
Reading books that have all the answers,
writing answers that have only questions.
Going into nature seeking divinity,
but riding the waves of uncertainty.
Only when I stopped and looked around,
and saw what was in front of me,
and realized the answers were here the whole time.
Going inside made the biggest impression
giving me everything I needed
for another dimension.

~ Mike Russell

Chapter 6

The Clairsenses

*Knowledge seekers know that there has to be
a better way to communicate than
through the physical senses and
are eager to learn new skills.*

Once you have protected and grounded yourself, you are now
open to use your intuitive senses, called the clairsenses, to
give you valid information. In your daily life, some of these
intuitive leaps spring from some senses more easily than
they do from others. For example, you may have clairvoyant
abilities, meaning that you can see past the physical world
and gather information from the colors, impressions, or
images you pick up on. Or you may be a person whose gut
feelings are never wrong; this would indicate that you have a
naturally strong clairsentient ability. Perhaps you are a
person who, despite not understanding how, often "knows"
details about a person you've just met, a situation going on
miles away, or a place you've never been. If so, you probably
have a natural leaning toward claircognizance. Are you a
person who can hear changes blowing in the wind? If so, you
have an inclination toward clairaudience.

You can also use your understanding of chakras to
identify others' clairsenses. According to a message received
from Archangel Raphael as it was channeled to Trisha, each
chakra has a corresponding primary clairsense (see table 2).
If you are looking at someone and notice chakras that stand
out in intensity and color, you will know which clairsenses
he or she is consciously or unconsciously using at that time.

For instance, if I look at a person and see a bright orange second chakra, one of this person's intuitive gifts is clairsentience. Any particularly bright, intensely colored chakra tells me that that chakra is the most active right at that moment.

Table 2: The Basic Chakras and their Clairsense Companions

	Chakra	Primary Clairsense	Area
1.	Root Chakra	Clairsentient	Tailbone and adrenals
2.	Sacral Chakra	Clairsentient	Sexual organs and lower abdomen
3.	Solar Plexus Chakra	Synoptic Sense Center	Digestive organs and immune system
	(central area that creates self-identity with all the clairsenses)		
4.	Heart Chakra	Clairaudient	Heart area includes respiratory
5.	Throat Chakra	Clairaudient	Throat, mouth, ears, and sinuses
6.	Third Eye or Brow Chakra	Clairvoyant	Eyes, pituitary, hypothalamus, and the base of the brain
7.	Crown Chakra	Claircognizant	Upper head, front of brain, and pineal gland

To determine which clairsense, or senses, you use every day without realizing it, try the following exercise with a partner. Remember that we are light and love and that to fully embrace our whole connection with Spirit, we need to utilize our clairsenses.

Determining Your Clairsenses

To do this exercise you need to have a willing partner. First, tell a memory of your childhood and then a memory of a recent event in your life. While you're telling your stories, have your partner watch your eye movements, head movements, and the way you tell the stories with your emotions. When your partner tells his or her stories, note the same about him or her. After you both have had an opportunity to tell your stories, discuss what you saw with your partner.

Remember that there are no hard-and-fast rules about identifying clairsenses, but the following are the basics for this exercise:

Eye movement
- Looks back and forth: clairaudient
- Looks up: clairvoyant
- Looks down: clairsentient
- Looks straight ahead: claircognizant

Head movement
- Side to side: clairaudient
- Down: clairsentient
- Up: clairvoyant
- Straight ahead: claircognizant

Using the following phrases
- I see or saw: clairvoyant
- I hear or heard: clairaudient
- I feel or felt: clairsentient
- I know or knew: claircognizant

Often a person will have two primary clairsenses that they use on a regular basis either consciously or subconsciously. This exercise gives someone a jumping-off point for knowing what his or her strengths might be. Interesting, no matter what your primary skill is, you can bring another skill like sight to confirm what your primary skill tells you. This gives you better discernment.

Freedom

To free yourself from earthly conviction,
that everything is done to you
outside of your reach.
Forgive, forgive, forgive
those around you.
Let go of the injustices done.
Forgive, forgive, forgive
your own feelings of superiority,
and let go of the need to be anything but spirit.
Forgive, forgive, forgive
the earth and beyond,
as we all search
for happiness within ourselves.

~ Mike Russell

Clairvoyance

*Knowledge seekers want to know how
it is possible to use something that they
cannot see through their physical eyes.*

I see it;
I believe it.
I see it;
I believe it.
I see it;
I believe it.

For more than two hundred years, clairvoyance meant "clear sighted." In the 1850s, the meaning of clairvoyance evolved to include a person's psychic gifts and seeing beyond the present, which it retains to this day. Basically, being clairvoyant is having the ability to see through the senses that are not tied to the physical form. People with this gift use it in many ways, including seeing colors, images, and sometimes moving images. This intuitive ability is centered on the third eye chakra and comprehending the light frequency of specific energy fields—the aura.

The Aura

The aura can be thought of as energy radiating off all matter whether it is alive or not. At the atomic level, all matter is made up of electrons and protons, which are constantly moving, and they create electrical and magnetic vibrations that can be seen. Matter that is alive vibrates at a higher level, so plants, animals, and humans have auras that can be seen more easily than things we consider not alive, such as a toaster, a car, or a computer. In actuality, everything is made up of the same electrons and protons, but because of their vibration rates some auras are easier to see than others. Take the human aura, for instance. It radiates in three dimensions, and a healthy person's aura can extend ten feet in all directions. The human aura gives any viewer the greatest opportunity to sense its presence.

When you see an aura, your physical eyes register light bouncing off an object. Your brain interprets the light data and holds the image of what is in front of you, yet you only perceive the light coming from it. When you are using your third eye, or mind's eye, to see beyond what your physical eyes are receiving, your peripheral vision picks up the light data and registers that information to the conscious mind.

Being clairvoyant is so much fun because our world is vivid. Life is not dull. Color dances off every person and every object around you. We all have at least one strong intuitive ability, and we are all different in our skills.

The color and intensity of the aura around a person or other specific living objects give a valuable understanding of physical, emotional, and mental well-being. We cannot fake our aura field. It shows our true intentions. Seeing auras gives you specific information for holding others with compassion and love.

We are all a spectrum of colors. Your brain has a way of analyzing information coming in. Now, when using your intuitive skills, your highest mind is gathering information and bringing it to your conscious mind, which knows colors, so a color-blind person can still see auras because doing so does not rely on the physical eyes. At first, you may not see a color but waves coming off your subject because you are sensing the energy field, which is a perfect place to be. If this happens, look deeper into the wave. All those steps are bringing clarity into your third eye.

Remember that people's energy and colors are moving, so one person will read another person a little bit differently. As a group, if we are sending the subject love energy then the field will change too.

Again, you are retraining your beliefs about your sight. As we see with our eyes, we are always internally assessing. When you are reading with your third eye, you are externally assessing everything in front of you. Just sensing light is perfect because it is the realization that we are all reading vibrations of light.

What a feeling does is anchor an outside effect because we are so accustomed to processing inward. The way of doing it is just the opposite. What I love about feelings is that in your peripheral vision, you will feel something, and then all of a sudden it happens out in front of you. Your mind is saying that it is safe to feel differently.

Feeling your way through it is like walking in the dark and suddenly having night vision. At first, we are just feeling our way through the dark; then our vision opens, and we can see in the dark. It is a beautiful entry into turning viewing on. The reality is that energy is always on. What you are doing when seeing an aura is bringing structure to what is always happening in front of you.

We discount so much that when we turn this gift on and use it, it helps bring our journey into focus. Sometimes it comes when you are not even looking. It can freak us out, so much so that in our mind, we determine that it will never happen again. We keep pushing this gift farther away from us. In the world of form, we are taught that logical consciousness is the equation for the success you are looking for. In reality, we are sentient beings who glean everything in an experience. So, that sight, that hearing, that knowing, and that feeling are really the jewels of where you are. If we all believe that we are thought forms expressed in this vehicle called the body, then we will recognize the energy and get ourselves out of just the physical existence.

When you are changing your beliefs consciously, you are going through that conscious place of reality of your mind. This is when doubts arise. Know that you are building the right pathways through the right placement to your highest mind and know that every time you make a new pathway over that bridge to your highest mind, it stays there, and every time you say no to an old pattern, it no longer is going to affect you as strongly. The more you do it, the more you can stay on that pathway and never feel as though you are falling back.

Remember that energetically, you are always moving forward, even though in your physical form you might be falling backward. Your mind always knows where you are. Because we believe in our bodies—that there is always a beginning, a middle, and an end—we experience doubt. So often, if you do not do something for years, you can pick it up fairly swiftly. If I am healing a pattern emotionally, I might fall back mentally, physically, or at the soul level, but not energetically.

Seeing and Reading an Aura

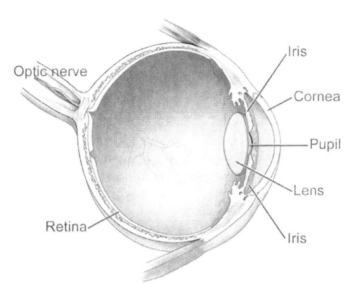

Iris

Optic nerve

Cornea

Pupil

Lens

Retina

Iris

Photo courtesy of the National Eye Institute,
National Institutes of Health

When we see, light comes in through the pupil, which is adjusted by the muscles of the iris. The light then affects the retina, activating the rods and cones in the outermost layer of the retina, which release chemicals that give you the colors and intensity of the light. This process allows you with practice to see the auric field around people, plants, trees, and animals and even around objects such as crystals and stones.

When working with clairvoyant abilities, many people want their third eye to act in the same manner as their physical eyes. Unfortunately, this desire brings more frustration than success. Energy around a person is in constant motion. When first receiving the light data from a person's energy field and instantly seeing the aura and its colors, the experience feels fleeting.

Because our eyesight can be trained to not see certain things, an important tool for viewing auras is your peripheral vision. Over time, the central part of the retina is damaged through normal use, as well as from all the artificial light sources. Take time and slowly allow your peripheral vision to gather the light data and with your mind's eye feel or know a color being projected before you.

Once that color is strong in your mind's eye, have your eyes register the light data of that color. Also you can soften what you see with your eyes by closing your eyelids halfway, strengthening your peripheral vision. Again, have your mind's eye resonate with a feeling or the knowledge of the color coming from a person in front of you. Allowing your conscious mind to create new pathways of seeing light data from different places of your eye gives your third eye chakra permission to stay open to see the world in a full spectrum of color.

A clear wall behind someone gives a clean surface to practice seeing auras easier. When you are looking at a person's aura, you are not concentrating on his or her physical body but on the surrounding energy bubble. Look at the area about a foot from the person's body. Slowly close your eyes halfway, allowing your peripheral vision to take in the light data. Once you feel, sense, or know a color around the person, slowly open your eyes to stimulate a triangulation between your third eye and your physical eyes. This triangle of collecting data gives strength to the wholeness of reading and interpreting the aura. Now use this triangle like a camera lens and bring the aura color into a three-dimensional view. The more you practice, the easier colors around animate life will appear.

Many times, viewing auras feels like you are receiving colors out of nowhere. This is because energy is constantly moving, and you are always picking up light data with your peripheral vision, making all the space around you and around others bring greater vividness to your life.

Expanding Your Auric Sight

To expand your auric sight, practice using your peripheral vision daily and use intention to increase your eyes' sensitivity to the vibrations beyond visible light. Through the increased visual sensation of light energy, and processing between the left and right hemispheres of the brain, a whole functioning of the brain occurs easier.

Peripheral Vision Exercise

Pair up with someone. Have one person hold different colored fabrics in each hand and raise and lower them in front of the other person, straight out to their sides in a windmill fashion while looking straight at the viewer. Have your partner note what he or she saw. Were there any aha moments? Did one eye see differently than the other? Were the colors the same on both right and left sides? If you are by yourself, you can do this by standing in front of a mirror. Take the colored fabrics and without trying to look at the colors you are holding, look straight ahead into the mirror. Focus on your forehead area. Now, slowly raise the colored fabrics that you are holding so that you can only see them by using your peripheral vision. Ask the same questions of yourself. You will be surprised with the colors that you can and cannot pick up and even whether you can see color. Sometimes you might find that one eye is picking up things completely different from the other eye. This exercise when practiced will strengthen that peripheral vision which is very important in developing clairvoyance. Have fun with it as you develop these skills.

Touch the Divine

Touching the Divine essence
is a reward to many.
Holding on to the spark of life,
and meriting this reward,
is the goal.
You can go through life
not touching the Divine,
which is perfect.
Never knowing
what is missing,
will not be known by you or
those around you.
Only when you step
forward and touch the Divine
with intention,
will you be free to set your own pace.

~ Mike Russell

Clairsentience

Knowledge seekers want to know
what it is like to feel an energy field
and how to interpret these feelings.

I feel it;
I realize it.
I feel it;
I realize it.
I feel it;
I realize it.

Clairsentience means "clear feeling." It relates to recurring physical and emotional feelings that you may have no knowledge of where or from whom they are coming; they are simply there. It is known as your gut feeling and signifies Divine Guidance. The main chakras involved in interpreting light energy are the root chakra and the second charka. Thus, this form of extrasensory perception is considered the most down to earth. Yes, your feelings and senses provide intuitive guidance regarding people, places, and events. For example, you have a strong sense of unease and discomfort while walking to the mailbox, and you intuitively glance behind you and find a person watching you.

Clairsentience comes strongly in three ways: gut feelings, physical sensations, and empathy. Gut feelings are strong in your second chakra area. You might have a sinking stomach feeling in advance of a dreaded event or an uplifting, excited feeling providing positive insight to a person, place, or event. Physical sensations start in your first and or second chakra and ripple throughout your physical body. Goosebumps, tickling, pressure, and the hair on your neck standing up all represent the gift of being clairsentient.

When I do energy work, I get impulses all the time from my Guides. I feel the right area on their body to be working at, and to facilitate the highest and best healing for that individual. The Divine connection is made beyond our physical forms to infuse us with the depth of sensing.

Empathy is an amazing intuitive gift. Empathy is the ability to pick up on the feelings of another person and to truly feel life as if in his or her skin. Living life as an antenna of other's is a double-edged sword. It allows you to know how to compassionately work with another creating win–win situations or if you are unskilled at interpreting the feelings you are receiving, you become a sponge absorbing and running emotions that are not your own. Highly sensitive people must become aware of your own feelings to feel comfortable in navigating the big, wide world around you. All intuitive gifts allow for clarity in living your truth in love and light.

Morning Feeling Report Exercise

After waking up in the morning, take time doing what I call the "Morning Feeling Report Exercise" to feel the day ahead of you. Feel your normal commute to work. Are you sensing the ease of flow with traffic? Are you getting anxious or becoming angry? How about taking a different route to work?

Once you arrive at work, feel the energy around your co-workers. Do they feel happy, sad, or frustrated? Can you add more joyful thoughts to bring more peace to what the day offers?

Now look at any meetings, gatherings, and conversations. How do these pending events make you feel? What strategies can you create to bring the best of you to this day? The expression of you provides the flow of all you have felt in your morning feeling report to have your "best day" ever!

Standing in Another's Shoes Exercise

All objects absorb energy from their owners, and by using clairsentient tools, you can tune into this residual energy field. This exercise involves using another person's shoes that he or she wears regularly. Close your eyes and hug the shoes to your gut area. Breathe deeply, connecting with the energy sensation from the shoes. Are you feeling a positive or negative vibe? Are you feeling happy, joyful, sad, confused, lost, or some other feeling? Share this information with the person. How accurate were you?

Feeling Your Chakras Exercise

This is an exercise for tuning into and reading your own energy. It is best to do this exercise when you have some knowledge of the chakra system (if you need to review the chakra system, see the beginning of this chapter. This exercise also helps to develop clairsentience because it makes you more sensitive to your emotions and feelings.

Here are the steps:

1. Lie down or sit comfortably.
2. Open each chakra, beginning with the root chakra. Visualize each chakra as a colored wheel spinning horizontally and bring your energy outward to about three feet outside of your body.
3. Then ask yourself, "How do I feel in this chakra?" Ask each chakra one by one. See if you get any sensations in your body or emotions that are connected to the chakras.

The first time I did this, I felt a sense of hollowness at the heart chakra, which is the center of love and self-love. That sensation told me that I was taking care of everyone except myself. At my throat chakra, which is the center of communication, I felt tight and constricted, and I remembered I had something to say to someone that I had suppressed.

To Know

Go to that place,
where it feels right.
Go to that place,
where the tingles
continue long after the event.
Go to that place of wonder,
where you were always told
it was your imagination.
To know,
is to accept the energy
that you were given to feel
long before you came.
To know is to allow yourself
the grace of being who you were
suppose to be and
who you want to be.

~ Mike Russell

Claircognizance

*Knowledge seekers want to know what
the most direct connection to Spirit is
and what it is like to claim the
right to know their divinity.*

I know it;
I grow it.
I know it;
I grow it.
I know it;
I grow it.

"Clear knowing," or claircognizance, is a form of extrasensory perception wherein a person acquires intuitive knowledge primarily by receiving verbal messages of another frequency or realm. The main chakra used here is the crown chakra. Messages you receive in other frequencies are usually heard internally with your inner ears.

With this clairsense, you know something is correct but may be unable to back up your statement with facts or explain how you came into that information. When you use this sense of intuition, you know what you are thinking or saying is true beyond any doubt. You consciously or unconsciously tap into the Divine Mind for inspiration, creativity, and innovation. When you experience claircognizance, it feels as if your idea or inspiration comes from a Higher Source and you feel compelled to put it into action.

Claircognizance is a form of extrasensory perception whereby a person acquires intuitive knowledge by receiving sudden, instant insights and understanding in their mind regarding a life situation or question. Claircognizance is primarily related to a strong, clear, healthy crown chakra and the ability to receive messages from your Spirit Guides in thought form. Claircognizance is the clearest connect to Source giving yourself or another knowledge of events that have happened in the past, present, or future. Many times, because the information received is a "knowing," discounting the validity of this information is easy. Trust is the biggest gift you can uphold when sharing and using all claircognizant knowledge.

Dictionary Game Exercise

To establish a free flow of thoughts, ideas, mental images and feelings, either by yourself or with others, open up a dictionary and randomly pick out a word. Say the word aloud three times. Now write down any knowledge and or insight that falls into your mind. With practice, you will be amazed at the information you just know.

The purpose of this game is to get you to let go of any stimulus that is around you through your normal senses, and just focus on what the word evokes to you through primarily your crown chakra. It tells you if you are making a connection through this clairsense. If you receive any information as if it is out there somewhere, then you know that claircognanizance is one of your strengths.

Angel Exercise

With yourself or with others, pick a beautiful Angel to bring information to you. Relax, take three deep breaths, and call out the Angel's name three times. Allow the Angel's essence to fill you up. See every cell in your body being, "pumped up" with the Angel's essence. Now open your crown chakra and receive any wisdom, insights, and knowledge. Write down in a journal all information received. With practice, your claircognizant skill will bring you valid understanding in your talents, purpose, and areas of forgiveness. You truly have a direct line to heaven.

The Leaf

The leaf hangs on,
with winter in full stride,
fluttering in the breeze,
and daring anyone to knock it off.
It strives to keep being, and
to be the last one standing
in its communication with Absolute Love.
It does not realize,
that just letting go,
brings it closer
than it has ever been
to the source it seeks.
Lessons are learned,
but oftentimes its faith
is not strong enough,
and so it holds on.

~ Mike Russell

Clairaudience

Knowledge seekers wonder about the sounds they hear
that they know did not come through their ears
and wonder about the possibilities.

I hear it;
I appear it.
I hear it;
I appear it.
I hear it;
I appear it.

Clairaudience, or "clear hearing," may refer not to actual perception of sound but to the impressions the inner mental ear picks up, similar to the way many people think words without having auditory impressions. But it may also refer to actual perception of sounds such as voices, tones, or noises that are not apparent to other humans or to recording equipment. For instance, a clairaudient person might claim to hear the voices or thoughts of the Spirits of persons who are deceased. It is like having a mental inner ear. This intuitive gift is about slowing down and listening deeply with your heart chakra, allowing the ripples of sounds to vibrate up into your inner ear. Your heart is your "true ear" of Spirit.

Often we learn to shut down our hearts, and the music of the heavens becomes white noise or memories of another time. The gift of truly listening opens clear communication with our Angels, Spirit Guides, and Higher Selves. Listen beyond your physical ears, and you will hear the full magic of sound. The best and easiest way to build your clairaudient intuitive skills is to take a listening break throughout the day. Now close your eyes and just listen. What noises are the easiest to pick out? Now listen deeper. Did you know even grass has a unique frequency, and hum? Can you hear the grass? Listening to birds is fun. Connect with their songs. Connect with the birds' heart. Connect with the birds' Spirit. What messages do you receive? I encourage you to practice listening, for all voices have wisdom to share!

Listening Discernment

To listen with discernment and receive the gems of wisdom is to recognize the highest vibration of truth you are hearing. Picking up vibrations without interference or distraction creates the connection of trust with yourself to fully manifest with Spirit. We are taught from an early age to tune out the noise around us and concentrate on hearing our parents, teachers, and all others we are told to respect. Their words become the laws unto us, which we follow in an autopilot mode. These conditioned patterns of listening are easily rewritten by actively listening to music. Vibration is truly what we were meant to listen to and to act from. To rewrite our listening patterns within our brains and hold discernment in our hearts, it begins with music you love. Pick a song that you love.

Play the song first and fall in love with this music. Feel your heart chakra fully embrace the music, and the vibrations of what you love. Hear the vibrations ripple up to your inner ear and connect your heart to your mind. Love the truth of hearing a piece of music of your choice. Your choice of what you love has rewritten a pathway of discerning hearing, which is your truth. Now listen to the song again actively, paying attention to only the words. Hear the words ripple up to your inner ear. Truly hear the magic of the words. You now have rewritten a pathway of discerning listening that makes the words hold truth to you.

Being involved in truthful action is a joyous dance. Finally, actively listen to the song one more time. Hear the beat and allow the beat to ripple out from your heart to your inner ear. Move to the beat that makes your heart ripple in love. You have fully rewritten the pathway of hearing and moving with Spirit. Your life will now flow easier with joy. The eternal music of creation is now yours to behold.

The Soul

The souls place,
brings the experience
of the past.
Fighting to give you the information
to exist here and now,
with more perfected calmness.
Given the opportunity
to do its job,
and talking from experience,
if only you will listen.
Given to repeat itself,
it does not care if you take its
information to heart or not.
It will remind you again and again,
and be very patient
in your quest for unity.

~ Mike Russell

Chapter 7

The Omega

*Knowledge seekers want to know how to
tie everything together and connect
all the different threads of the Spirit.*

Through this book, you have been connecting deeper and deeper with your Divine essence and renewing your contact with Absolute Love. Now going into your Higher Self and being guided through Spirit can bring you a greater appreciation and trust of how generous Spirit is. With each experience of the wholeness of love, you are snuggled into the perfection of you as the holy creator. Each chapter has brought you back to you and to the full power of Absolute Love.

You know that you have done a good job with this information because of the way you act and feel. You may smile more, or feel that your life is being guided somehow beyond just your day-to-day reality. Lights will be brighter, colors will be bolder, and you may find yourself laughing more. I like to say that I tune into the Trisha channel every day. I get excited to wake up and see what I am going to do that day.

You actually have excitement about your life. Even if you have had some experience before that might have been fearful, it is just more intriguing now, a story line that enables you to see why you might have had this written into your journey because it is definitely bringing out a lesson without getting so into the pain of it. You just move through things so much differently.

Remember how vast our subconscious mind is. The conscious mind is just the tip of the iceberg. Ninety percent of the unconscious mind is below the surface. So, when you are looking at something and an issue comes up, your first reaction might be only to the tip of the iceberg. We think that an issue is healed, but that painful story that triggered your reaction says is that, on an unconscious level, there really has to be a better way, that there has to be a better way we are calling forth the Divine essence to co-create love that is eternal.

The gift of you to fully be you in your free choice to be Absolute Love is the gift of freedom you seek. You are the pivot point of all you are. You are the key to heaven on earth. Blessings.

Acknowledgments

This book has been the result of many years of study by Trisha Michael. Throughout the years and the many ups and downs of daily living, a story line developed. This story line involved a childhood of extraordinary spiritual connection that continued over her informative years through college. Marriage and children added to the story line, and although spiritual matters were placed in the background because they needed to be, the envelope of love from her Guides always protected her on her path of discovery.

It took the partnership of Trisha and Mike to spark the strong spiritual outflow from Archangel Raphael who helped guide and create the T Michael Healing Arts Clinic in Beaverton, Oregon, and the offerings that it is known for today.

Of course, none of this would have been possible without Trisha's initial visitation and acceptance that there had to be another way. The stepping-stones were laid and the course was set to create the story presented here.

We would like to thank everyone involved in either our clinic or our classes who helped us test the techniques presented here. We would like to say a special thank you to Melissa Armour and Elizabeth Armour, the mighty editing and organizing wing for the materials that helped so much in our classes. We would have seriously been lost without their help. Thanks also go out to Nancy Adams and Denise Hoffman for helping us move to a better product through their ideas.

It takes many people to create a story line that stretches over a lifetime. We thank all those involved in our lives that helped lead us here. You never do it alone.

We would like to acknowledge our publisher, Sharon Lund of Sacred Life Publishers, who took inexperienced writers under her wings and gracefully guided us through the process. We want to thank Miko Radcliffe, graphic design artist, for taking our book cover to a new level. We would also like to thank our editor, Wendy Jo Dymond, who took our manuscript and made it flow into a graceful work that brought the "Stairway to Absolute Love" to life. Special thanks goes out to Ardel Chisholm our graphic designer from LincMedia Design for all the great graphics for this book and to Garrett and Sara Russell of GBR Productions for being our photographer and crew.

And finally, how do you thank the Angels involved in this project except by stating that we are both truly humbled by the opportunity to have their encouragement over both of our lifetimes and to guide us to this point, always knowing with their patience and love, that this is exactly where we were supposed to end up. No one knows another person's alpha and omega or beginning or ending because it involves free will, and that is decided by the person who sets his or her own story before coming here. People create their own contracts and carry them out. What I know is that we created a contract long ago through many lifetimes, knowing full well that it would lead right here, right now. And as you read this book, your free will is carrying out your own contract to interplay with our story line.

Our hope is that you found the time spent to be helpful, that your intuitive skills have been triggered and can now grow, and that you continue the story line that you so desire.

About the Authors

Trisha Michael and Mike Russell

Trisha Michael has lived in Oregon for the past twenty years. She made her journey to the West Coast from Upstate New York to finish her premed degree and become a healer. Her life changed instantly when an Angel appeared that set her on a course of studying different modalities within the healing arts. Over the years, she has become a Reiki master and Angelic Spiritual Coach. Trisha has been inspired by Archangel Raphael to take his lessons into the community through special sessions of profound communication and thoughtful reflection. She is a gifted energy practitioner with many other related skills. She continues to reflect to all that "Love Is Enough" and strives to bring peace and understanding to all her clients.

In the spring of 2010, Archangel Raphael decided that the time was right to encourage Trisha to participate more fully in a relationship that would involve channeling his messages. He came as a result of her partnership with Mike, which allowed them to participate together in a project of spreading his main message that "Love Is Enough." This partnership has developed into not only a healing business but also the spreading of Archangel Raphael's message through various means of communication in print and video.

Thanks to Archangel Raphael's connection and encouragement, the T Michael Healing Arts Clinic continues to expand and grow through its participating healers and special events. Trisha's connection to Archangel Raphael continues to strengthen and grow in love with the intention that through his helpful messages, all are informed, and feel his special energy.

Mike Russell grew up knowing that there was more to the world than what he was noticing through his physical senses, but he had no way to understand those things that were considered to be out of the ordinary in a 1960s world. With his father serving in the US Air Force, he and his family moved every three years to a different part of the world, opening his eyes to the smallness of this planet while at the same time learning from his English mother that ghosts do exist and it was okay to talk about spiritual matters.

It wasn't until years later as he developed his interest in all things related to Spirit and the death of his wife, that he was plunged head first into the deep waters of intuition.

Through Spirits encouragement, he joined forces to write a book with Trisha about her expansive knowledge and created a wonderful and loving partnership with the help of Archangel Raphael.

Intuition has played an important role in his life but now with this foundation created through partnership, Mike now has a platform to pursue and offer this information to all those that are interested, and as it meets the tender and funny way that he is referred to by Archangel Raphael as the "newspaper delivery boy," he feels honored to take this mantle on and is proud to be able to get the word out.

CPSIA information can be obtained
at www.ICGtesting.com
Printed in the USA
FFOW01n1329240716
26183FF